the great pepper *cookbook*

THE **ULTIMATE GUIDE** TO CHOOSING AND COOKING WITH PEPPERS

OxmoorHouse

welcome

The aromas and flavors captive in every fresh and dried pepper evoke instant memories from every corner of one's personal culinary template. The Great Pepper Cookbook from Melissa's Produce is more than a cookbook, more than an encyclopedia, more than a guide. It's a passport to understanding the most universal ingredient of the New World.

As the largest global distributor of fresh and dried peppers, Melissa's is equipped to share information about more than 30 types of peppers and chile peppers, ranging from sweet bell peppers to blistering bhut jolokia chile peppers and, for the fearless, the scorpion chile pepper, considered one of the hottest on Earth. Here, you'll find all you need to know about peppers and chile peppers, including seasonality, personality, and availability.

In addition to delicious recipes, charts and notes are included to guide you through the Scoville heat units scale, so you'll know just how hot the pepper is before it reaches your tongue, and you can adjust the heat according to your desires. Peppers and chile peppers are integral to the Melissa's family, a privately owned and cared for business founded by Sharon and Joe Hernandez.

www.melissas.com   (800) 588-0151   f 🐦 MelissasProduce

Is it hot in here?

While flavor (rather than heat) was our main focus when creating these recipes, any dish made with fresh or dried chile peppers will have some degree of heat. Here's our guide so you can feel the burn—or not!

MELLOW 🌶

Just a touch of heat to make you feel a little warm inside.

ZIPPY 🌶🌶

Just sassy enough to make you peel off a few layers of clothing.

KICKIN' 🌶🌶🌶

Don't call the fire department, but have a tall glass of water on hand just in case.

contents

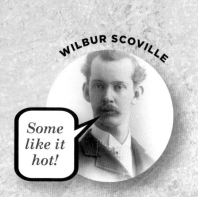

WILBUR SCOVILLE

Some like it hot!

Veggie Sweet Mini
0

Bell Pepper
0

Padron
100–1,000

100

Shishito
100–1,000

Cherry Bell
100–3,500

Hatch
250–30,000

Hatch
(dried)
1,000–10,000

Banana Wax
500–4,500

the
scoville scale

Jalapeño
3,500–11,000

5,000

Pasilla Negro
4,000–8,000

Chipotle
7,000–15,000

7,500

Tepin
40,000–70,000

50,000

Cayenne
8,000–18,000

Manzano
10,000–20,000

De Arbol
15,000–25,000

Serrano
15,000–30,000

Japones
15,000–35,000

Pequin
50,000–75,000

Thai
50,000–100,000

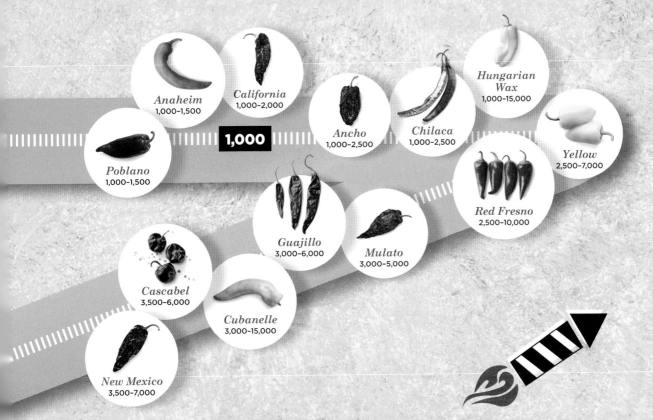

Anaheim
1,000–1,500

California
1,000–2,000

Ancho
1,000–2,500

Chilaca
1,000–2,500

Hungarian Wax
1,000–15,000

Yellow
2,500–7,000

Poblano
1,000–1,500

1,000

Red Fresno
2,500–10,000

Guajillo
3,000–6,000

Mulato
3,000–5,000

Cascabel
3,500–6,000

Cubanelle
3,000–15,000

New Mexico
3,500–7,000

A little more than a century ago, Wilbur Scoville developed the Scoville Organoleptic Test to determine the range of capsaicinoid compounds (Scoville heat units) of each chile pepper, from the mildest pepper that clocks in at 0 SHU to fiery chiles that register in the millions. The question is...how hot will you go?

Habanero
100,000–200,000

Habanero (dried)
200,000–300,000

300,000

Red Savina Habanero
300,000–576,000

Savina Ruby Hot Habanero (dried)
300,000–576,000

Bhut Jolokia (fresh and dried)
575,000–1 million

Scorpion (fresh and dried)
1.4 million–2 million

Melissa's guide to fresh and dried peppers and chile peppers

Chile peppers, some of the earliest crops to be grown, add wonderful flavor and spice to dishes all over the world. Our guide includes the most widely available fresh and dried chile peppers in the United States, as well as the bell peppers and veggie sweet mini peppers that are so important to our cuisine.

When selecting fresh peppers and chile peppers, avoid any that are limp, shriveled, and have soft spots or bruises. Store them in a plastic bag, at room temperature for up to five days or in the refrigerator for up to ten days. Be sure to store each type of chile pepper separately, since the oils from their heat can transfer to other produce.

Chile peppers have also long been dried and smoked, changing and intensifying their flavor and making them available year round. The difference in flavor is so marked that a different name is usually in order—for example, smoked jalapeño chile peppers are called chipotle chile peppers. Store dried chile peppers in an airtight container in a cool, dry, dark place for up to six months.

FRESH

ANAHEIM

SHU: 1,000–1,500 (Mild)
SEASON: Year Round
OTHER NAMES: New Mexico, Colorado
SUBSTITUTIONS: New Mexico, Hatch (mild)

The Anaheim chile pepper is narrow, about 6–8 inches long, and pale to glossy green. Named after the southern California city where it was originally grown, the Anaheim is favored because of its sweet, mild flavor. Choose firm, glossy chiles.

BHUT JOLOKIA
(BOOT jo-LO-kee-uh)

SHU: 575,000–1,000,000
(Extremely Hot to Insanely Hot)
SEASON: July–October
OTHER NAMES: Ghost, Naga Jolokia
SUBSTITUTIONS: Red Savina, Habanero, Scorpion

The bhut jolokia chile pepper is about the size of an adult's thumb. This chile, which hails from Assam, India, is commonly known as the "ghost chile," and is one of the hottest on the planet. Use this chile very sparingly—its intense heat can overpower both the dish and the diner! The bhut jolokia has a fruity smell and a mildly acidic taste. Choose bright reddish-orange, glossy chiles that are firm.

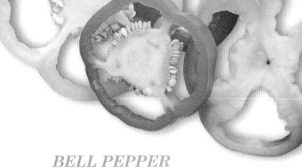

BANANA WAX

SHU: 500–4,500 (Mild to Medium)
SEASON: Year Round
OTHER NAMES: Banana, Yellow Wax, Wax
SUBSTITUTIONS: Cubanelle,
Cherry Bell, Hungarian Wax

The banana wax chile pepper is narrow, about 4–7 inches in length, and a lightly translucent creamy yellow. While it usually has a sweet, mild flavor, some varieties can be quite hot. Choose firm, yellow, glossy chiles.

BELL PEPPER
(green, red, yellow, orange)

SHU: 0 (No Heat)
SEASON: Year Round
OTHER NAME: Sweet Pepper
SUBSTITUTION: Veggie Sweet Mini Peppers

The bell pepper is a round pepper, characterized by its thick flesh, bright skin, and fairly sweet flavor. Bell peppers come in a variety of flavors and colors. Green is the most popular color, followed by red, which has the sweetest flavor; both are easy to find year round. Yellow has the mildest flavor, and along with orange, is most common in summer. Choose peppers that are firm and brightly colored; avoid peppers that appear shriveled, dull, or pitted.

CAYENNE
(green and red)

SHU: 8,000–18,000 (Medium to Hot)
SEASON: July–September
OTHER NAMES: Guinea Spice,
Cow Horn, Red Hot
SUBSTITUTIONS: Thai, Serrano

The cayenne chile pepper, common in powders and sauces but less common in its fresh form, is a long, skinny, curvy chile that ends in a pointed tip; it ranges from 4–8 inches in length, and can grow up to 1 inch in thickness. The mature red chiles are spicier than the green, and both are used in many cuisines. Choose brightly colored, glossy chiles that are firm.

CHERRY BELL

SHU: 100–3,500 (Mild)
SEASON: Year Round
OTHER NAME: Cherry
SUBSTITUTIONS: Cubanelle,
Banana Wax, Manzano

The cherry bell chile pepper is about 1–2 inches in diameter and usually deep red in color; the round shape and color make this chile resemble a cherry, thus the name. The cherry bell has a great tangy-sweet flavor, and even chiles that are somewhat spicy retain a sweet flavor. Due to its thick skin, this chile is rarely dried, but is often pickled. Choose red, glossy chiles that are firm.

FRESH

CHILACA

SHU: 1,000–2,500 (Mild)
SEASON: Almost Year Round
(dependent on weather)
OTHER NAME: None
SUBSTITUTION: Poblano

The chilaca chile pepper is the size and shape of a large cayenne chile pepper, measuring an average of 6 inches long (although some can grow 9 inches or longer!). It is a dark to blackish green in color, and its shiny surface has undulating vertical ridges. It has a slightly sweet flavor, but a hot variety also exists. Choose chiles that are smooth, shiny, and firm.

CUBANELLE

SHU: 3,000 (Mild); up to 15,000 (Hot)
for less common varieties
SEASON: Year Round
OTHER NAMES: Italian, Dominican Aji
SUBSTITUTIONS: Banana Wax, Cherry Bell

The Cubanelle chile pepper is 4–6 inches long, and ranges from a waxy light yellow to greenish color. This chile is a classic frying pepper, and has a sweet, mild flavor. The Cubanelle chile is most popular in its immature stage, when it is yellow with a thin skin and thick flesh. As it matures, the Cubanelle turns orange-red and then vivid red. The heat rises as the chile matures. Choose crisp, yellow, glossy chiles; avoid limp and shriveled chiles.

HUNGARIAN WAX

SHU: 1,000–15,000 (Mild to Hot)
SEASON: Year Round
OTHER NAMES: Hungarian Yellow Wax,
Hungarian Banana Wax
SUBSTITUTION: Banana Wax

The Hungarian wax chile pepper, which is very similar to the banana wax chile pepper, is about 6–8 inches in length, grows up to 2 inches wide, and is a translucent creamy yellow color. It has a thin skin with a thick flesh; picked at an immature stage, the Hungarian wax has a sweet flavor varying from warm to moderately hot. Choose crisp, yellow, glossy chiles.

JALAPEÑO

SHU: 3,500–11,000 (Mild to Hot)
SEASON: Year Round
OTHER NAME: None
SUBSTITUTIONS: Yellow, Red Fresno, Serrano

The jalapeño chile pepper is typically 2–4 inches long and 1 inch thick. Larger, milder varieties also exist, with some as long as 5 inches. All have a rounded tip, glossy skin, and thick flesh. The jalapeño ranges in color from pale to dark green, with some red available in summer. Named after Jalapa, the capital of Veracruz, Mexico, the jalapeño is among the most popular and commonly available chiles in the U.S. Choose chiles that are firm.

HABANERO
(orange, red savina)

SHU: Orange: 100,000–200,000
(Extremely Hot); Red Savina: 300,000–
576,000 (Extremely Hot)
SEASON: Orange: Year Round;
Red Savina: August–September
OTHER NAME: Havana
SUBSTITUTIONS: Scotch Bonnet, Bhut Jolokia

The orange habanero chile pepper is the most common variety of habanero; it is lantern-shaped and reaches about 2 inches long and up to 1¾ inches in diameter. The orange habanero has a fierce, intense heat, and is considered one of the hotter chile varieties grown in the U.S. The orange habanero is 30–50 times hotter than the jalapeño chile pepper; the red Savina habanero, which is only available for a limited time throughout the growing season, is 65 times hotter than the jalapeño. Choose chiles with skin that is shiny, smooth, and unblemished and a scent that is fresh and slightly floral.

HATCH

SHU: 250–30,000 (Mild to Very Hot)
SEASON: August–September
OTHER NAMES: New Mexico,
New Mexico Hatch
SUBSTITUTIONS: New Mexico, Anaheim,
California, Banana Wax, Poblano

The Hatch chile pepper is long with a pointed end—it looks very much like a curvy Anaheim chile—and can grow 6–9 inches long, and up to 2 inches wide. The Hatch has a meaty flesh, and can range from mild to hot, depending upon the variety. Authentic New Mexican Hatch Chiles are named after the original growing area in Hatch, New Mexico. Choose bright green, glossy chiles that are firm.

MANZANO

SHU: 10,000–20,000 (Hot)
SEASON: Year Round
OTHER NAMES: Tree, Rocoto, Locoto
SUBSTITUTION: Cherry Bell

The manzano chile pepper is round, and is about the size of a walnut. The manzano can be one of three colors: orange (most common), red, or yellow. Some varieties can be as hot as 50,000 SHUs or greater. Prized for its very thick skin and meaty interior, the manzano chile is unusual in that it has black seeds, unlike any other variety of chile. Choose chiles that are firm with no bruises.

PADRON

SHU: 100–1,000 (Mild)
SEASON: Year Round
OTHER NAME: La Coruña
SUBSTITUTION: Shishito

The padron chile pepper ranges from 2–4 inches in length, and has wrinkly skin. The padron is generally mild in flavor—similar to the heat of an Anaheim chile pepper—but occasionally, a fiery pepper randomly occurs, sometimes even on the same bush. Sometimes confused with the longer shishito chile pepper, this small, thin-skinned chile was traditional to the Galicia region of Spain, and is commonly grown in Morocco as well. Choose chiles whose skin and stem are bright in color; avoid chiles with blemishes, cuts, or dark spots.

FRESH

POBLANO
(pasilla)

SHU: 1,000–1,500 (Mild)
SEASON: Year Round
OTHER NAMES: Pasilla, Relleno
SUBSTITUTIONS: Hatch, Anaheim, Chilaca

The poblano chile pepper is broad shouldered and V-shaped, averaging 5–8 inches in length and about 3 inches wide, with very thick flesh. Dark green, with splashes of purple-black color, the poblano has a rich, sweet-yet-astringent flavor with a mild heat (although the occasional chile approaches medium heat). Used in a variety of delicious traditional Latin dishes, the poblano is among the most popular chiles used in Mexico. Choose firm, heavy, smooth-skinned chiles that are glossy.

RED FRESNO

SHU: 2,500–10,000 (Mild to Medium)
SEASON: Year Round
OTHER NAME: Cera
SUBSTITUTIONS: Jalapeño, Yellow

The red Fresno chile pepper is 2–4 inches long and about 1½ inches in diameter. The red Fresno is very similar in shape and heat to the jalapeño chile pepper, and is often mistaken for a red jalapeño, though the red Fresno has wider shoulders, thinner flesh, and a pointed tip. Choose brightly colored, glossy chiles that are firm.

SHISHITO

SHU: 100–1,000 (Mild)
SEASON: Year Round
OTHER NAME: Japanese
SUBSTITUTION: Padron

The shishito chile pepper is typically about 2–4 inches long and about ½ inch wide; it is slender, curvy, and wrinkly with rounded ends. The name of this chile is derived from the Japanese word for "lion's head," which the tip of the shishito is said to resemble. The bumpy skin matures from light lime green to dark, wrinkled red; the shishito is harvested before it ripens to red, and should be consumed while still green. The flavor is sweet, mild, and refreshingly "green." Choose chiles that are bright green with no red tinge.

THAI
(red and green)

SHU: 50,000–100,000 (Very Hot)
SEASON: Year Round
OTHER NAMES: Asian, Bird's Eye
SUBSTITUTIONS: Serrano, Cayenne

The Thai chile pepper is small and slim with a pointed end, usually 1–3 inches in length. Its thin flesh has many tiny seeds, but don't let its seemingly unthreatening size be deceiving. Commonly used in Southeast Asian cuisine, this blazing hot chile has a seriously strong, lingering heat. One of several small chiles referred to as "bird's eye" chiles, it is popular in both Thai and Indian cuisines. Choose glossy chiles that are firm.

SCORPION

SHU: 1,400,000–2,000,000
(Insanely Hot)
SEASON: Year Round
OTHER NAMES: Trinidad, Moruga, Butch
SUBSTITUTION: Bhut Jolokia

The scorpion chile pepper is small and round, less than 1 inch in length and width. It is red to orange in color, and has a little horn-like hook characteristic of a scorpion tail—and a sting to match. Touted as one of the hottest chile peppers in the world by Guinness World Records, it packs a fruity, fiery bite (it's 100 times hotter than a jalapeño chile pepper). Choose brightly colored, glossy chiles that are firm.

SERRANO

SHU: 15,000–30,000 (Hot to Very Hot)
SEASON: Year Round
OTHER NAME: Sinaloa
SUBSTITUTIONS: Thai, Jalapeño, Cayenne

The serrano chile pepper is about 2–3 inches long, finger-shaped, and bright to dark green, although some are harvested after turning orange or even red. It has a sudden, intense bite with an herbal flavor that doesn't linger. Choose chiles that are firm, shiny, and evenly colored.

VEGGIE SWEET MINI PEPPERS

SHU: 0 (No Heat)
SEASON: Year Round
OTHER NAMES: Mini Sweet Peppers, Mini Peppers, Vine Sweet Mini Peppers
SUBSTITUTION: Bell Peppers

The veggie sweet mini pepper is small and bright red, orange, or yellow. It features thick flesh, a sweet taste, and good texture. This virtually seedless pepper has a surprisingly mild flavor; it looks like a chile pepper but tastes similar to a very sweet bell pepper. Choose bright peppers with a glossy finish that are plump and have a firm texture.

YELLOW

SHU: 2,500–7,000 (Mild to Medium)
SEASON: Year Round
OTHER NAMES: Guero, Caribe, Santa Fe
SUBSTITUTIONS: Red Fresno, Jalapeño

The yellow chile pepper is about 2–4 inches long, yellow, and medium hot with a sharp flavor and firm texture. Similar to the Hungarian wax chile pepper, the yellow chile is medium fleshed and slightly sweet with a sharp flavor, pleasant crunch, and spicy aroma. Choose chiles that have a solid yellow color with no pits or red blemishes.

FRESH PEPPER PREP

Roasting and charring peppers and chile peppers brings out deeper sweetness and adds a hint of smoke to bridge heat and flavor. Peppers and chiles should be washed and patted dry before roasting, and kept whole with stems intact. Remember to wear rubber gloves when handling hotter chiles!

ROAST IN THE OVEN

1 Preheat oven to 425°F. Rub peppers with cooking oil and arrange in a single layer on a foil-lined baking sheet.

2 Roast 15 to 25 minutes, turning several times, until all sides are lightly blistered.

CHAR UNDER THE BROILER

1 Preheat broiler to high. Rub peppers with cooking oil and arrange in a single layer on a foil-lined baking sheet.

2 Broil 5 to 10 minutes, turning several times, until all sides are darkly blistered.

Note: When handling any hot chile pepper, you should be cautious. It's mandatory that you wear rubber gloves and, once you're done, wash your hands thoroughly using soapy hot water to avoid skin and eye irritation. Keep all chile peppers away from children during the handling process.

CHAR ON THE GRILL

1 Preheat a charcoal or gas grill to medium-high heat. Rub peppers with cooking oil and arrange in a single layer on the grill rack.

2 Grill 5 to 10 minutes, turning several times, until all sides are darkly blistered.

CHAR OVER AN OPEN FLAME

1 Heat gas burner to medium-high heat. Char pepper 5 to 10 minutes, using heat-proof tongs, until all sides are darkly blistered.

2 Place a metal cooling rack over gas burner to char multiple peppers.

COOL AND PEEL

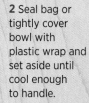

1 Place charred peppers in a plastic bag or a heatproof bowl or dish.

2 Seal bag or tightly cover bowl with plastic wrap and set aside until cool enough to handle.

3 Gently peel away charred skin before removing seeds and stems.

REMOVE SEEDS AND STEMS

1 Remove stems by breaking open the pepper with hands or using a knife.

2 Shake out seeds.

ANCHO

SHU: 1,000–2,500 (Mild)
DRIED VERSION OF: Poblano
SUBSTITUTIONS: Mulato, Pasilla Negro

The Ancho chile pepper, a dried poblano chile pepper, is usually about 3–5 inches long; it's wide on top ("ancho" means wide in Spanish), tapering to a rounded, slightly pointed end. Brick red to a deep brown or almost black, this is the sweetest of the dried chiles; it's full-bodied but relatively mild, although some can have a hint of heat. It has slight chocolate flavor notes, and has been a common ingredient in Southwestern-influenced dessert recipes lately.

BHUT JOLOKIA
(ghost)

SHU: 575,000–1,000,000 (Insanely Hot)
DRIED VERSION OF: Bhut Jolokia (Ghost)
OTHER NAME: Ghost
SUBSTITUTIONS: Savina Ruby Hot Habanero, Habanero, Trinidad Scorpion

The bhut jolokia chile pepper, commonly known as the "ghost chile pepper," is about the size of an adult's thumb. The hottest natural (non-crossbred) chile pepper out there, it has a slow heat that takes a few minutes to hit your mouth, as well as a faint fruity flavor.

CALIFORNIA

SHU: 1,000–2,000 (Mild)
DRIED VERSION OF: Anaheim
SUBSTITUTIONS: Hatch (Mild), New Mexico

Among the most popular and commonly available chiles in the U.S., the California chile has a distinct sweet, slight-to-medium heat and is indispensable to making red chile sauce. It imparts a full-bodied chile flavor when added to Latin dishes, and is often used in tied chains or garlands, many of which are decorative.

CASCABEL

SHU: 3,500–6,000 (Medium)
OTHER NAME: Chile Bola
SUBSTITUTION: Guajillo

The Cascabel chile pepper measures about 1½ inches in diameter, is a dark reddish-brown, and is sometimes called the "ball" or "bell" chile because it is smooth and round. It tastes smoky with an acidic bite and a low-to-medium level of heat, and it can have a hint of wood-toned flavor. When this Mexican chile is dried, the seeds break loose, and so it gets its name from the rattling sound it makes when shaken (in Spanish, "cascabel" means "little bell").

CHIPOTLE

SHU: 7,000–15,000 (Medium to Hot)
DRIED VERSION OF: Jalapeño
SUBSTITUTION: Pasilla Negro

The chipotle chile pepper is a smoked, dried jalapeño chile pepper that has a meaty, smoky, spicy heat and deep, richly unique flavor that makes it the most popular dried hot chile. The chipotle's heat varies widely due to the broad heat spectrum of its fresh counterpart, but for the most part, it tends toward the hot side. Unlike many other fresh chiles, jalapeños are not as popularly enjoyed when they turn red— yet the opposite holds true for drying, because only red jalapeños get turned into chipotles.

DE ARBOL

SHU: 15,000–25,000 (Hot)
OTHER NAME: Tree
SUBSTITUTIONS: Cayenne, Japones

The de arbol chile pepper is similar to a cayenne chile pepper, but is larger and longer. This bright red chile is primarily used in powdered form to make sauces; its astringent spiciness leaves a strong impression and a lingering heat on the tongue. The de arbol chile keeps its bright red hue after drying, so it is often found in decorative wreaths instead of in the pantry.

HATCH

SHU: Mild: 1,000–10,000 (Mild to Hot)
DRIED VERSION OF: Hatch
SUBSTITUTIONS: New Mexico, Guajillo, Pasilla Negro

The Hatch chile pepper, grown exclusively in Hatch, New Mexico, is considered to be one of the most flavorful chiles in the world. With a surprisingly rich taste, it has a back note of lemon peel, and is available in both mild and spicy versions.

JAPONES

SHU: 15,000–35,000 (Hot to Very Hot)
OTHER NAME: Asian
SUBSTITUTION: De Arbol

The japones chile pepper, which is a native of Mexico but is also used in Asian cuisine, is a small yet flavorful chile with medium-high heat.

GUAJILLO

SHU: 3,000–6,000 (Mild to Medium)
SUBSTITUTIONS: New Mexico, Hatch, Cascabel

The guajillo chile pepper is a long, dark red chile popularly used to make tamale sauce in Mexico. It has a fairly mild heat range, though it can approach spicy. It is better rehydrated than ground.

HABANERO
(habanero, savina ruby hot)

SHU: *HABANERO* 200,000–300,000 (Extremely Hot); *SAVINA RUBY HOT* 300,000–576,000 (Extremely Hot)
DRIED VERSION OF: Orange Habanero, Red Savina Habanero
SUBSTITUTION: Bhut Jolokia (Ghost)

The habanero chile pepper, named after the city of Havana, is one of the hottest dried chiles out there. The small, acorn-shaped chile has thin flesh and, behind the formidable heat, carries hints of tropical fruit and berry flavors. The Savina Ruby Hot habanero is a dried red habanero variety that has a hotter Scoville reading than the common habanero.

MULATO

SHU: 3,000–5,000 (Mild to Medium)
SUBSTITUTIONS: Ancho, Pasilla Negro

The mulato chile pepper, a cousin of the Ancho chile pepper and sometimes mislabeled as an Ancho, has a full-bodied but relatively mild heat. Slightly smaller than the Ancho, it is nearly black when dried, but it has similar chocolate-like undertones and has a meaty texture when rehydrated.

NEW MEXICO

SHU: 3,500–7,000 (Medium)
SUBSTITUTIONS: Hatch, California

The New Mexico chile pepper is slightly smaller than its brother, the Hatch chile pepper, and imparts a wonderful, light yet rounded flavor. Even dried, its "green" notes come through in cooking.

DRIED

PASILLA NEGRO

SHU: 4,000–8,000 (Medium)
OTHER NAME: Negro
DRIED VERSION OF: Chilaca
SUBSTITUTIONS: Ancho, Mulato, Hatch, Chipotle

The pasilla negro chile pepper, a dried chilaca chile, has a rich, smoky flavor with moderate heat (not to be confused with the fresh poblano, which is sometimes called a pasilla chile pepper). Rehydrated and minced, it combines surprisingly well with fruits in a fruit-based salsa.

PEQUIN

SHU: 50,000–75,000 (Very Hot)
OTHER NAME: Flea Pepper
SUBSTITUTION: Tepin

The pequin chile pepper is a small, red, highly potent chile with a light, sweet, smoky flavor; a hint of citrus; and a deep, fiery, transient heat. This tiny pepper was a favorite of the Aztec Indians who referred to it as the "flea pepper."

TEPIN

SHU: 40,000–70,000 (Very Hot)
OTHER NAME: Bird's Eye
SUBSTITUTION: Pequin

The tepin chile pepper is a wild version of the pequin chile pepper, and is smaller and rounder—it's like a berry that has a searing heat and a hint of clove and spice. Ground tepin chile is a great substitute for other ground red pepper, since it has a more powerful heat.

TRINIDAD SCORPION

SHU: 1,400,000–2,000,000 (Insanely Hot)
DRIED VERSION OF: Trinidad Scorpion
SUBSTITUTION: Bhut Jolokia (Ghost)

The Trinidad scorpion chile pepper packs a flavor bite that should be taken very seriously and in small quantities. For perspective, this chile is more than 100 times hotter than a jalapeño chile pepper, and it was listed as the hottest dried chile in the Guinness World Records in 2012.

DRIED PEPPER PREP

Toasting dried peppers and chile peppers in a skillet or in the oven intensifies their flavor. Once toasted, remove the stems and seeds before grinding in a spice grinder or rehydrating toasted whole peppers in hot water. Store dried peppers in an airtight container and keep in a cool, dry, and dark place for up to six months. Remember to wear rubber gloves when handling hotter chiles!

TOAST IN THE OVEN

1 Preheat oven to 300°F. Wipe peppers to remove any dust or debris.

2 Arrange peppers in a single layer on a baking sheet. Bake 3 to 4 minutes until peppers are fragrant.

TOAST UNDER THE BROILER

1 Preheat broiler to high. Wipe peppers to remove any dust or debris.

2 Arrange dried peppers in a single layer on a baking sheet. Broil 3 to 5 minutes, turning several times, until peppers are fragrant.

Note: When handling any hot chile pepper, you should be cautious. It's mandatory that you wear rubber gloves and, once you're done, wash your hands thoroughly using soapy hot water to avoid skin and eye irritation. Keep all chile peppers away from children during the handling process.

TOAST IN A DRY SKILLET

1 Wipe peppers to remove any dust or debris. Tear peppers open and shake out seeds.

2 Heat skillet over medium-high heat; press open peppers with a flat spatula. Toast 2 to 3 minutes until peppers are fragrant.

GRIND IN A SPICE GRINDER

1 Tear toasted dried peppers into small pieces and place in a spice grinder.

2 Grind until desired consistency.

REMOVE SEEDS AND STEMS

1 Remove stems by breaking open the pepper with hands or using a knife.

2 Shake out seeds.

REHYDRATE IN HOT WATER

1 Wipe peppers to remove any dust or debris.

2 Place toasted peppers in a large bowl and add boiling water to cover.

3 Place a small bowl or plate on top of peppers to keep them submerged. Soak for 15 to 20 minutes, until soft and pliable.

4 Drain well and pat gently with paper towels to remove any excess water.

» CRAB-HATCH
CHILE JALAPEÑO
POPPERS

appetizers, snacks, *and* drinks

Hatch

FRESH

Jalapeño

FRESH

CRAB-HATCH CHILE JALAPEÑO POPPERS 🌶🌶

Carefully pick through crabmeat to clean it, gently feeling for any bits of shell with fingertips to avoid crumbling the juicy chunks of meat.

PREP TIME: **30 MIN.** / TOTAL TIME: **45 MIN.** / SERVES: **16 (1 POPPER)**

Make Ahead

To save time, prepare the jalapeños and crab mixture up to one day ahead. Store in separate tightly covered containers and refrigerate.

4 cups shredded mozzarella cheese (about 1 pound)
½ pound lump crabmeat, cleaned
3 fresh Hatch chile peppers, roasted, peeled, stems and seeds removed, and diced (about ⅓ cup)
16 large fresh jalapeño chile peppers (about 1½ pounds), halved

1. Preheat oven to 400°F. Line a baking sheet with foil; lightly spray with cooking spray. In a large bowl, gently combine cheese, crabmeat, and Hatch chile.

2. Carefully remove seeds and veins from jalapeño chile halves. Spoon crabmeat mixture evenly into jalapeño chile halves. Arrange on prepared baking sheet. Bake at 400°F until jalapeño chiles just start to get tender and cheese browns, about 7 to 10 minutes. Serve.

Calories 132; **fat calories 56; total fat 6g; sat fat 4g; cholesterol 25mg; sodium 225mg; total carbohydrates 10g; fiber 2g; sugars 5g; protein 13g; vitamin A IUs 28%; vitamin C 344%; calcium 22%; iron 5%**

MINI CRISPY FISH TACOS 🌶🌶

In addition to cod, you can use barramundi, tilapia, or pollock.

PREP TIME: **40 MIN.** / TOTAL TIME: **1 HR. 30 MIN.** / SERVES: **15 (1 TACO)**

Ancho

|||||||||||||||||||||||||

DRIED

|||||||||||||||||||||||||

¾ cup canola oil
15 (6-inch) corn tortillas
1 cup water
1 dried ancho chile pepper, stem and seeds removed
1 cup whole milk
1 teaspoon baking powder
½ teaspoon salt
½ teaspoon freshly ground black pepper
1 garlic clove, minced
1 cup all-purpose flour
1 pound fresh whitefish (such as cod) fillets, cut into 15 (about 1-inch-wide) strips
1 large onion, finely chopped (about 2 cups)
4 tomatoes, finely chopped (about 2½ cups)
1 cup chopped fresh cilantro
3 limes, cut into wedges

1. In a large saucepan, heat oil to 375°F. Fry tortillas one at a time until golden brown, about 1 minute per tortilla; bend each to form a taco-shell shape immediately upon removing from hot oil. Drain on rack over paper towels.
2. In a small saucepan, combine 1 cup water and chile. Bring just to boiling. Reduce heat; simmer until chile is soft, about 5 minutes.
3. Place chile and chile water, milk, and next 4 ingredients (through garlic) in a blender*;

process until smooth. Pour into a large shallow bowl. Slowly whisk in flour until a smooth batter forms.
4. Return oil to 375°F. Dip fish strips in batter; fry 3 strips until golden brown and cooked through, about 3 to 5 minutes. Drain on paper towels. Repeat procedure with remaining fish strips and batter.
5. Place 1 fish strip in each taco shell; top each evenly with onion, tomato, and cilantro. Garnish with lime wedges. Serve.

*Note: Be cautious when blending hot foods; the contents expand rapidly, causing a risk of scalding. To be safe, before blending, remove center piece of blender lid (to allow steam to escape), secure lid on blender, and place a towel over opening in lid (to avoid splatters).

Calories 200; **fat calories** 80; **total fat** 9g; **sat fat** 1g; **cholesterol** 15mg; **sodium** 40mg; **total carbohydrates** 22g; **fiber** 3g; **sugars** 4g; **protein** 9g; **vitamin A IUs** 15%; **vitamin C** 10%; **calcium** 4%; **iron** 4%

Simple Swap

For a quicker version of this recipe, use purchased taco shells.

Manzano

FRESH

CRAB-STUFFED CUCUMBER CUPS 🌶

Cucumber cups make a fun serving vessel for this party appetizer.

PREP TIME: **35 MIN.** / TOTAL TIME: **45 MIN.** / SERVES: **40 (1 CUCUMBER CUP)**

Make Ahead

Prepare the crab filling ahead of time for a quick party appetizer.

4 large cucumbers, peeled and ends removed
⅛ teaspoon salt
4 ounces cream cheese, softened (about ½ cup)
½ cup sour cream
3 limes, zested and juiced (about 2 tablespoons zest and ⅓ cup juice)
1 pound lump crabmeat, cleaned
½ cup fresh cilantro leaves, finely chopped
3 garlic cloves, minced
3 fresh manzano chile peppers (about 12 ounces), roasted, peeled, stems and seeds removed, and diced
2 ribs celery, finely chopped
1 ear fresh corn, grilled or roasted, kernels removed (about ⅔ cup)
Chile powder (optional)
Lemon-peel curls (optional)
Cilantro leaves (optional)

1. Cut cucumbers crosswise into ¾-inch slices. Using a melon baller, remove most of the middle of each cucumber without going all the way through to the bottom, forming each into a cup. Sprinkle evenly with salt.

2. In a large bowl, stir together cream cheese, sour cream, zest, and juice until smooth. Gently fold crabmeat and next 5 ingredients (through corn) into cream cheese mixture. Spoon crabmeat mixture evenly into cucumber cups. Garnish with chile powder, lemon-peel curls, and cilantro leaves, if desired. Serve.

Calories 40; **fat calories** 15; **total fat** 1.5g; **sat fat** 1g; **cholesterol** 15mg; **sodium** 100mg; **total carbohydrates** 3g; **fiber** 1g; **sugars** 1g; **protein** 3g; **vitamin A IUs** 4%; **vitamin C** 10%; **calcium** 2%; **iron** 0%

SPICY STUFFED MUSHROOMS 🌶🌶

Red Fresno

FRESH

You can use cremini or baby portobellos in place of button mushrooms if you prefer.

PREP TIME: **20 MIN.** / TOTAL TIME: **1 HR. 15 MIN.** / SERVES: **6 (2 MUSHROOMS)**

12 large button mushrooms, stems trimmed, removed, and reserved
2 tablespoons extra-virgin olive oil
1 small sweet onion, finely diced (about 1 cup)
1 garlic clove, minced
1 rib celery, finely diced (about ⅓ cup)
1 fresh red Fresno chile pepper, stem and seeds removed, finely diced
¼ cup panko (Japanese breadcrumbs)
4 tablespoons unsalted butter, melted (¼ cup)
½ cup grated Parmesan cheese (about 2 ounces)
Salt
Freshly ground black pepper

1. Preheat oven to 350°F. Line a baking sheet with foil. Arrange mushroom caps on prepared baking sheet, open side up. Lightly coat mushrooms with cooking spray. Bake at 350°F for 10 minutes. Cool until can be handled, about 10 minutes.

2. Finely dice reserved mushroom stems. In a large skillet, heat oil over medium-high heat. Add onion; cook until browned, stirring occasionally, about 10 minutes. Add mushroom stems, garlic, celery, and chile to skillet; cook until stems are softened, about 3 minutes. Remove from heat; stir in breadcrumbs, butter, and cheese. Cool 10 minutes.

3. Spoon mushroom-onion mixture evenly into mushroom caps. Bake at 350°F until completely heated through, about 7 to 8 minutes. Sprinkle with salt and black pepper to taste. Serve.

Calories 180; **fat calories** 130; **total fat** 15g; **sat fat** 7g; **cholesterol** 30mg; **sodium** 180mg; **total carbohydrates** 8g; **fiber** 1g; **sugars** 2g; **protein** 6g; **vitamin A IUs** 6%; **vitamin C** 10%; **calcium** 15%; **iron** 2%

Heat It Up!
Ramp up the heat by doubling the amount of Fresno chiles used.

Anaheim

FRESH

CHILE AND CHEESE EMPANADAS 🌶

For a colorful variation, use an assortment of red, yellow, and green bell peppers in place of the Anaheim chiles.

PREP TIME: **35 MIN.** / TOTAL TIME: **3 HR. 35 MIN.** / SERVES: **14 (1 EMPANADA)**

Simple Swap
Purchase refrigerated pizza dough if short on time.

1 cup warm water (about 110°F)
1 teaspoon active dry yeast (¼-ounce package)
1 teaspoon sugar
3 cups all-purpose flour
1 tablespoon salt
¼ cup extra-virgin olive oil, divided
1 large egg
1 tablespoon water
3 fresh Anaheim chile peppers, roasted, peeled, stems and seeds removed, and diced
½ cup shredded sharp cheddar cheese (about 2 ounces)
⅓ cup grated Parmesan cheese (about 1.5 ounces)

1. In a bowl, stir together 1 cup warm water, yeast, and sugar until yeast and sugar are dissolved. Let yeast mixture stand in a warm place until it foams, about 5 to 10 minutes.
2. In the bowl of a mixer fitted with a dough hook, combine flour and salt. Starting at lowest speed, mix while adding yeast mixture until a tacky dough begins to form, about 3 minutes. Gradually increase speed to medium; mix until dough gathers into a ball, about 2 minutes. Add 2 tablespoons oil; mix 1 minute.
3. Turn dough out onto a lightly floured surface; knead until

smooth and elastic. Form into a ball; transfer to a bowl oiled with remaining 2 tablespoons oil, turning dough to coat completely. Cover with plastic wrap or a damp towel; let rise in a warm place (85°F), free from drafts, until doubled in size, about 1 hour.
4. Preheat oven to 350°F. Line a baking sheet with parchment paper. Roll out dough into 28 (4-inch) rounds, each about ⅛ inch thick. In a bowl, whisk together egg and 1 tablespoon water. Using a pastry brush, paint edges of dough with half of egg mixture. Top each of 14 dough rounds evenly with chile and cheddar cheese; top with remaining dough rounds. Crimp edges with a fork to seal. Paint tops with remaining half of egg mixture; sprinkle evenly with Parmesan cheese. Arrange on prepared baking sheet.
5. Bake at 350°F until completely cooked through and golden brown, about 30 minutes. Serve.

Calories 190; **fat calories** 70; **total fat** 8g; **sat fat** 3g; **cholesterol** 25mg; **sodium** 590mg; **total carbohydrates** 23g; **fiber** 1g; **sugars** 3g; **protein** 6g; **vitamin A IUs** 10%; **vitamin C** 130%; **calcium** 8%; **iron** 8%

CHEDDAR-CHILE-LIME BREADSTICKS 》》

Serve these tangy sticks with a big bowl of chili.

PREP TIME: **30 MIN.** / TOTAL TIME: **1 HR. 5 MIN.** / SERVES: **12 (1 BREADSTICK)**

2	cups all-purpose flour
2	tablespoons sugar
1½	teaspoons baking powder
1½	teaspoons salt, divided
3	tablespoons all-vegetable shortening
½	cup ice-cold water
2	limes, juiced (about ¼ cup)
½	cup finely grated Parmesan cheese, divided (about 2 ounces)
¼	cup finely shredded sharp cheddar cheese (about 1 ounce)
4	dried japones chile peppers, stems and seeds removed, finely ground (about 1 tablespoon)

Olive oil

1. Preheat oven to 350°F. Lightly spray 2 baking sheets with cooking spray. Process flour, sugar, baking powder, and ½ teaspoon salt in a food processor until combined. Add shortening; process until mixture resembles coarse meal, about 10 (1-second) pulses. With the food processor on, slowly add ½ cup cold water and lime juice. Add ¼ cup Parmesan cheese and all the cheddar cheese and process until mixture forms a smooth ball, about 10 minutes.

2. Turn dough out onto a lightly floured surface; roll out into a rectangle ¼ inch thick. Using a pizza cutter or knife, cut dough lengthwise into 12 even strips. Using hands, roll strips back and forth to form into long, round sticks. Twist sticks by grasping each end and twisting in opposite directions.

3. Arrange in a single layer on prepared baking sheets (sides should not touch). Combine chile and remaining 1 teaspoon salt in a bowl; sprinkle evenly over sticks. Bake at 350°F until firm and completely cooked through, about 15 minutes. Brush sticks evenly with oil; sprinkle evenly with remaining ¼ cup Parmesan cheese. Bake at 350°F until golden, about 5 minutes. Cool on wire racks. Serve.

Calories 100; **fat calories** 40; **total fat** 4.5g; **sat fat** 1.5g; **cholesterol** 5mg; **sodium** 180mg; **total carbohydrates** 12g; **fiber** 0g; **sugars** 2g; **protein** 3g; **vitamin A IUs** 2%; **vitamin C** 2%; **calcium** 6%; **iron** 2%

Japones

DRIED

Kitchen Savvy

Make a double batch of the dough and freeze half for up to a month. Let thaw about 8 hours before preparing and baking.

CHEESY BREADSTICKS 🌶🌶

If you thought you had to knead, rise, stretch, rise, and knead again to treat your guests to home-baked breadsticks, guess again. With just three ingredients and 25 minutes, you can have cheesy, peppery sticks fresh from the oven.

PREP TIME: **10 MIN.** / TOTAL TIME: **35 MIN.** / SERVES: **10 (2 BREADSTICKS)**

Serrano

FRESH

- 2 puff pastry sheets, fully thawed if frozen
- 2 fresh serrano chile peppers, stems and seeds removed, finely diced
- ¾ cup grated Parmesan cheese, divided (about 3 ounces)

1. Preheat oven to 400°F. Lightly spray 2 baking sheets with cooking spray. Unfold puff pastry sheets onto a lightly floured surface. Sprinkle evenly with chiles and ½ cup cheese. Lightly press chile and cheese into puff pastry with a rolling pin. Using a pizza cutter or knife, cut pastry lengthwise into 20 (½-inch) strips. Twist sticks by grasping each end and twisting in opposite directions.
2. Arrange in a single layer on prepared baking sheets (sides should not touch). Spray sticks lightly with cooking spray and sprinkle evenly with remaining ¼ cup cheese. Bake at 400°F until golden brown, about 15 minutes. Cool on wire racks. Serve.

Calories 200; **fat calories** 130; **total fat** 14g; **sat fat** 4.5g; **cholesterol** 5mg; **sodium** 300mg; **total carbohydrates** 18g; **fiber** 1g; **sugars** 2g; **protein** 6g; **vitamin A IUs** 0%; **vitamin C** 10%; **calcium** 6%; **iron** 8%

Kitchen Savvy
For the best results, let the pastry defrost slowly in the refrigerator.

SWEET, SMOKY, SPICY PARTY NUTS 🌶️🌶️

This addictive mix makes a great holiday snack. Experiment with mix-ins such as pretzel pieces, cereal, or even crushed candy cane pieces.

PREP TIME: **10 MIN.** / TOTAL TIME: **1 HR. 40 MIN.** / SERVES: **12 (½ CUP)**

2	large egg whites
1	tablespoon sugar
5	dried japones chile peppers, stems and seeds removed, ground (about 1 tablespoon)
1½	cups purchased smoked almonds
1½	cups purchased butter toffee peanuts
1½	cups shelled pistachios
1½	cups cashew halves
1	tablespoon canola oil

1. Preheat oven to 275°F. Line a baking sheet with foil; lightly spray with cooking spray. In a large bowl, whisk together egg whites, sugar, and chile. Add nuts; gently toss together. Stir in oil.

2. Arrange nuts in a single layer on prepared baking sheet. Bake at 275°F until nuts are lightly toasted, stirring every 10 minutes, about 30 minutes.

3. Transfer baking sheet to a wire rack; stir nut mixture once more, spreading out. Cool completely. Serve.

Calories 280; **fat calories** 193; **total fat** 21g; **sat fat** 5g; **cholesterol** 3mg; **sodium** 107mg; **total carbohydrates** 19g; **fiber** 3g; **sugars** 10g; **protein** 8g; **vitamin A IUs** 3%; **vitamin C** 1%; **calcium** 5%; **iron** 10%

Make Ahead

Make and store this irresistible snack up to three days in advance... but you'd better hide the container!

Veggie Sweet Mini

FRESH

Bhut Jolokia

DRIED

PEPPER, ASPARAGUS, AND MUSHROOM SKEWERS 》》》

Use large stalk asparagus instead of the thinner "pencil" asparagus.

PREP TIME: **15 MIN.** / TOTAL TIME: **55 MIN.** / SERVES: **20 (1 SKEWER)**

Cool It Down!

The bhut jolokia (ghost) chile pepper is one of the hottest dried chiles on the market. For more timid palates, substitute dried de arbol chile.

20 fresh veggie sweet mini peppers, halved lengthwise, stems and seeds removed

10 fresh asparagus stalks, washed and trimmed, each stalk cut into 4 pieces

20 small button mushrooms, halved

20 8-inch bamboo skewers, soaked in water for 30 minutes

1½ cups grated Parmesan cheese (about 6 ounces)

1 cup panko (Japanese breadcrumbs)

1 teaspoon granulated garlic

1 dried bhut jolokia (ghost) chile pepper, stem and seeds removed

2 large eggs, beaten

1. Preheat oven to 450°F. Line 2 baking sheets with foil; lightly spray each with cooking spray. Thread 2 mini pepper halves, 2 asparagus pieces, and 2 mushroom halves alternately onto a skewer. Repeat procedure with remaining mini pepper halves, asparagus pieces, mushroom halves, and skewers.

2. In a large shallow bowl, combine cheese and breadcrumbs. Grind garlic and chile in a spice grinder until finely ground. Stir spice mixture into breadcrumb mixture.

3. Dip skewer in egg and dredge in breadcrumb mixture. Place on prepared baking sheet. Repeat procedure with remaining skewers and breadcrumb mixture (there will be some breadcrumb mixture remaining). Bake at 450°F until golden brown, about 10 minutes. Serve.

Calories 50; **fat calories** 30; **total fat** 3g; **sat fat** 2g; **cholesterol** 30mg; **sodium** 160mg; **total carbohydrates** 2g; **fiber** 0g; **sugars** 1g; **protein** 5g; **vitamin A IUs** 2%; **vitamin C** 15%; **calcium** 10%; **iron** 2%

DEVILISH DEVILED EGGS 🌶🌶

For even more devilish fun, garnish eggs with extra ground japones chile and thinly sliced chives.

Japones

DRIED

PREP TIME: **15 MIN.** / TOTAL TIME: **47 MIN.** / SERVES: **20 (1 DEVILED EGG)**

10 large eggs, room temperature
½ cup mayonnaise
1 teaspoon yellow mustard
3 sun-dried tomatoes, finely chopped
2 dried japones chile peppers, stems and seeds removed, ground
1 Meyer lemon, juiced (about 3 tablespoons)
Salt

1. In a large saucepan, heat water over medium-high heat just to boiling, about 5 minutes. Using a large slotted spoon, gently lower eggs into boiling water. Return water to boiling; cook 12 minutes. Cover; remove from heat and let stand 5 minutes. Run cold water over eggs until cool enough to handle, about 5 to 10 minutes.

2. Peel eggs; halve lengthwise. Remove yolks and transfer to a medium bowl. Mash yolks with a fork. Stir in mayonnaise, next 4 ingredients (through juice), and salt to taste. Spoon yolk mixture evenly into egg white halves. Serve or refrigerate, covered, up to 3 days.

Calories 80; **fat calories** 60; **total fat** 7g; **sat fat** 1.5g; **cholesterol** 95mg; **sodium** 75mg; **total carbohydrates** 1g; **fiber** 0g; **sugars** 0g; **protein** 3g; **vitamin A IUs** 4%; **vitamin C** 2%; **calcium** 2%; **iron** 2%

» MANGO AND
CHILE-GLAZED
PARTY WINGS

MANGO AND CHILE-GLAZED PARTY WINGS 🌶🌶

Ancho

DRIED

PREP TIME: **20 MIN.** / TOTAL TIME: **1 HR. 35 MIN.** / SERVES: **10 (ABOUT 3 WINGS)**

- 4 dried ancho chile peppers, stems and seeds removed, divided
- 2 large eggs
- 1 cup all-purpose flour
- 1 teaspoon salt
- 1 teaspoon freshly ground black pepper
- 8 tablespoons unsalted butter (½ cup)
- ½ cup plus 1 tablespoon extra-virgin olive oil, divided
- 4 pounds chicken wings with drumettes
- 3 cups frozen mango chunks
- 1½ cups water
- ½ cup packed brown sugar

1. Grind 1 ancho chile in a spice grinder until finely ground. In a shallow bowl, lightly beat eggs. In a separate shallow bowl, combine flour, salt, black pepper, and ground ancho chile.

2. Lightly spray a baking dish with cooking spray. In a large straight-sided sauté pan, heat butter and ½ cup oil to 375°F. Dip wings in egg mixture and dredge in flour mixture; fry, in batches, until golden brown, turning once, about 7 to 10 minutes. Place wings in prepared baking dish. Return oil to 375°F between batches.

3. Preheat oven to 350°F. Place remaining ancho chiles, remaining 1 tablespoon oil, mango, 1½ cups water, and sugar in a blender; process until smooth. Pour mango mixture over wings. Cover baking dish with foil; bake at 350°F until wings are completely cooked through, basting frequently with mango mixture, about 30 minutes. Serve.

Calories 770; **fat calories** 380; **total fat** 43g; **sat fat** 14g; **cholesterol** 195mg; **sodium** 390mg; **total carbohydrates** 58g; **fiber** 1g; **sugars** 20g; **protein** 36g; **vitamin A IUs** 80%; **vitamin C** 25%; **calcium** 2%; **iron** 15%

BACON-WRAPPED GRILLED ASPARAGUS 🌶🌶🌶

Trinidad Scorpion

DRIED

PREP TIME: **5 MIN.** / TOTAL TIME: **30 MIN.** / SERVES: **4 (1 ASPARAGUS BUNDLE)**

- 4 slices thick-cut hickory-smoked bacon
- 16 stalks asparagus, trimmed (about ¾ pound)
- 1 dried Trinidad scorpion chile pepper, stem and seeds removed, ground

1. Preheat oven to 350°F. Line a baking sheet with foil and set a wire rack on top. Arrange bacon on prepared rack. Bake at 350°F until bacon is partially cooked, about 5 to 7 minutes.

2. Preheat grill to medium-high heat. Wrap each slice of bacon around 4 stalks of asparagus; sprinkle evenly with chile. Place bundles on grill rack; grill directly over heat, turning often, until bacon is crisp and asparagus cooked through and slightly tender, about 7 to 10 minutes. Serve.

Calories 60; **fat calories** 20; **total fat** 2.5g; **sat fat** 1g; **cholesterol** 5mg; **sodium** 100mg; **total carbohydrates** 6g; **fiber** 2g; **sugars** 2g; **protein** 4g; **vitamin A IUs** 15%; **vitamin C** 20%; **calcium** 2%; **iron** 2%

Red Fresno

FRESH

RED HOT LEMONADE 🍋🍋

This recipe makes a tasty Key limeade, too: Just use ¾ cup fresh Key lime juice (you'll need about 20 limes) instead of lemon juice. For a fun presentation, float thinly sliced red Fresno chile peppers and lemon slices in each glass.

PREP TIME: **10 MIN.** / TOTAL TIME: **15 MIN.** / SERVES: **8 (ABOUT ¼ CUP)**

½ gallon cold water
4 lemons, juiced (about ¾ cup)
1 fresh red Fresno chile pepper, stem and seeds removed, finely diced
1 cup sugar

1. In a pitcher, stir together all ingredients until sugar dissolves completely, about 3 to 5 minutes. Pour over ice. Serve.

Calories 100; **fat calories** 0; **total fat** 0g; **sat fat** 0g; **cholesterol** 0mg; **sodium** 0mg; **total carbohydrates** 27g; **fiber** 0g; **sugars** 26g; **protein** 0g; **vitamin A IUs** 2%; **vitamin C** 30%; **calcium** 0%; **iron** 0%

Hatch

FRESH

BANANA-MANGO-CHILE AGUA FRESCA 🍋🍋

Aguas frescas are classic liquid refreshers, popular from Mexico down to South America. They are typically simple, containing fruit blended with sugar water.

PREP TIME: **20 MIN.** / TOTAL TIME: **25 MIN.** / SERVES: **4 (ABOUT 1½ CUPS)**

2 cups water
1 cup whole milk
¼ cup sugar
1 large fresh mango, peeled, pitted, and chopped
1 banana
1 fresh Hatch chile pepper, roasted, peeled, stem and seeds removed, and diced

1. Place all ingredients in a blender; process until smooth. Serve.

Calories 160; **fat calories** 20; **total fat** 2.5g; **sat fat** 1g; **cholesterol** 5mg; **sodium** 30mg; **total carbohydrates** 35g; **fiber** 2g; **sugars** 30g; **protein** 3g; **vitamin A IUs** 25%; **vitamin C** 150%; **calcium** 8%; **iron** 2%

>> RED HOT LEMONADE

LEMONGRASS-GINGER COOLER

LEMONGRASS-GINGER COOLER "

Jalapeño

FRESH

Sweeten with a little honey, if desired, and garnish with extra-thinly sliced jalapeño chile.

PREP TIME: **10 MIN.** / TOTAL TIME: **1 HR. 40 MIN.** / SERVES: **6 (ABOUT 1⅓ CUPS)**

6 cups water
5 ounces fresh ginger, thinly sliced
1 large piece fresh lemongrass, trimmed, split lengthwise, and chopped (4 ounces)
1 fresh jalapeño chile pepper, stem and seeds removed, thinly sliced

1. In a large saucepan, combine all ingredients; bring just to boiling. Reduce heat; simmer 30 minutes. Strain into a pitcher through a fine mesh strainer, discarding solids. Cool 1 hour. Pour over ice. Serve.

Calories 5; **fat calories** 0; **total fat** 0g; **sat fat** 0g; **cholesterol** 0mg; **sodium** 0mg; **total carbohydrates** 1g; **fiber** 0g; **sugars** 0g; **protein** 0g; **vitamin A IUs** 0%; **vitamin C** 4%; **calcium** 0%; **iron** 1%

Make Ahead
Steep the ginger and lemongrass the day before.

FIERY TANGERINE FREEZE "

Red Fresno

FRESH

Serve this creamy delight at your next pool party.

PREP TIME: **10 MIN.** / TOTAL TIME: **15 MIN.** / SERVES: **8 (ABOUT 1 CUP)**

4½ pounds tangerines, juiced (about 3 cups)
1¼ cups whole milk
1 cup cold water
½ cup sugar
2 teaspoons pure vanilla extract
1 fresh red Fresno chile pepper, stem and seeds removed, finely diced
10 ice cubes

1. Place all ingredients except ice cubes in a blender; process until smooth. With blender on, drop in 1 ice cube at a time; process until smooth and frothy. Serve.

Calories 210; **fat calories** 20; **total fat** 2g; **sat fat** 1g; **cholesterol** 5mg; **sodium** 20mg; **total carbohydrates** 49g; **fiber** 5g; **sugars** 42g; **protein** 3g; **vitamin A IUs** 35%; **vitamin C** 120%; **calcium** 15%; **iron** 2%

Tepin

DRIED

CHILE-BERRY AGUA FRESCA 🌶🌶

The combination of fresh berries and piquant tepin chile peppers is especially refreshing on a hot summer day. Stick to strawberries and blueberries or mix and match your favorite berries.

PREP TIME: **10 MIN.** / TOTAL TIME: **15 MIN.** / SERVES: **8 (1½ CUPS)**

Heat It Up!

Spice up this drink even more with crushed dried habanero chile pepper.

½ 16-ounce container strawberries, hulled
1 cup blueberries
2 cups cold water
½ cup fresh lime juice
6 tablespoons sugar
4 dried tepin chile peppers, crushed, divided
1 tablespoon Kosher salt
Lime wedges
5 cups sparkling or soda water

1. Place strawberries, blueberries, 2 cups cold water, juice, sugar, and half of chile in a blender; process until smooth and sugar is dissolved.

2. In a shallow bowl, combine salt and remaining half of chile. Rub rims of 8 serving glasses with lime wedges; dip rims in salt mixture, shaking off excess.

3. Fill prepared glasses with ice; pour strawberry mixture over ice until half full. Top each glass with sparkling water. Garnish with lime wedges. Serve.

Calories 70; **fat calories** 5; **total fat** 0g; **sat fat** 0g; **cholesterol** 0mg; **sodium** 300mg; **total carbohydrates** 18g; **fiber** 2g; **sugars** 14g; **protein** 1g; **vitamin A IUs** 6%; **vitamin C** 70%; **calcium** 2%; **iron** 2%

Serrano

FRESH

KICKED-UP SMOOTHIES 🌶🌶

Garnish this delicious tropical smoothie with thinly sliced serrano chile peppers.

PREP TIME: **5 MIN.** / TOTAL TIME: **10 MIN.** / SERVES: **4 (ABOUT 1½ CUPS)**

2 cups low-fat vanilla frozen yogurt
1 cup fresh strawberries, hulled
1 cup fresh pineapple chunks
1 banana
1 fresh serrano chile pepper, stem and seeds removed, finely diced

1. Place all ingredients in a blender; process until smooth. Serve.

Calories 200; **fat calories** 45; **total fat** 5g; **sat fat** 3g; **cholesterol** 15mg; **sodium** 45mg; **total carbohydrates** 37g; **fiber** 2g; **sugars** 26g; **protein** 4g; **vitamin A IUs** 4%; **vitamin C** 80%; **calcium** 10%; **iron** 2%

Kitchen Savvy

Any pre-cut frozen fruit can be used instead of fresh fruit.

Bhut Jolokia

FRESH

POTENT PIÑA COLADAS 🌶🌶🌶

Traditional piña coladas are made with alcohol. If you are missing the rum, add 1 cup before blending.

PREP TIME: **5 MIN.** / TOTAL TIME: **10 MIN.** / SERVES: **6 (ABOUT 1 CUP)**

1¾ cups fresh pineapple chunks
1½ cups crema de coco
1½ cups ice cubes
½ fresh bhut jolokia (ghost) chile pepper, stem and seeds removed
½ cup macadamia nuts, finely chopped

1. Place pineapple, crema de coco, ice cubes, and chile in a blender; process until smooth. Pour over ice; top evenly with nuts. Serve.

Calories 387; **fat calories** 187; **total fat** 21g; **sat fat** 13g; **cholesterol** 0mg; **sodium** 30mg; **total carbohydrates** 50g; **fiber** 2g; **sugars** 45g; **protein** 2g; **vitamin A IUs** 4%; **vitamin C** 40%; **calcium** 1%; **iron** 4%

**KICKED-UP
SMOOTHIES**

» STRAWBERRY-BANANA-MANGO SLUSHERS

STRAWBERRY-BANANA-MANGO SLUSHERS 🌶

Manzano

FRESH

PREP TIME: **5 MIN.** / TOTAL TIME: **10 MIN.** / SERVES: **6 (ABOUT 1 CUP)**

1 pint fresh strawberries, hulled and frozen

2 cups frozen mango chunks (about 4 Manila or 3 standard)

3 bananas

½ fresh manzano chile pepper, stem and seeds removed, chopped

1. Place all ingredients in a blender; process until slushy and not quite smooth. Serve.

Calories 113; **fat calories** 3; **total fat** 0g; **sat fat** 0g; **cholesterol** 0mg; **sodium** 0mg; **total carbohydrates** 29g; **fiber** 6g; **sugars** 29g; **protein** 1g; **vitamin A IUs** 10%; **vitamin C** 93%; **calcium** 1%; **iron** 3%

SUGAR AND SPICE COCOA 🌶🌶

New Mexico

DRIED

Make a nondairy version by using rice milk in place of the whole milk.

PREP TIME: **5 MIN.** / TOTAL TIME: **17 MIN.** / SERVES: **6 (ABOUT ¾ CUP)**

4 cups whole milk

2 dried New Mexico chile peppers, stems and seeds removed

1 vanilla bean

½ cup semi-sweet chocolate chips

14 "pinwheel" peppermint candies, crushed (about ⅓ cup)

1. In a medium saucepan, combine milk and chiles. Split vanilla bean lengthwise; scrape seeds into milk mixture. Add pod to pan.
2. Bring milk mixture just to a scald (when small bubbles surface around the edge) over low heat, about 5 minutes. Add chips and candies; cook until completely dissolved, stirring constantly, about 8 minutes. Remove chiles and vanilla bean pod. Serve.

Calories 273; **fat calories** 93; **total fat** 10g; **sat fat** 6g; **cholesterol** 17mg; **sodium** 70mg; **total carbohydrates** 39g; **fiber** 1g; **sugars** 27g; **protein** 6g; **vitamin A IUs** 20%; **vitamin C** 0%; **calcium** 20%; **iron** 3%

Simple Swap

If you don't have vanilla bean pods in your pantry, use 2 teaspoons vanilla extract instead.

OPEN-FACED BREAKFAST SANDWICHES

breakfast *and* brunch

Cayenne

FRESH

OPEN-FACED BREAKFAST SANDWICHES 〟〟〟

Feel free to substitute ground black pepper for the ground cayenne if you're worried about heat.

PREP TIME: **20 MIN.** / TOTAL TIME: **4 HR. 30 MIN.** / SERVES: **4 (1 SANDWICH)**

8   ounces honey
2   fresh cayenne chile peppers, stems and seeds removed, finely diced, divided (about 2 tablespoons)
4   thick slices whole-wheat French bread
2   tablespoons unsalted butter, divided
½   cup creamy goat cheese (about 4 ounces)
4   large eggs
Salt
Ground cayenne pepper

1. In a glass container, combine honey and half of cayenne chile; seal tightly and let sit 4 hours or overnight.

2. Toast bread; spread each toast slice with 1 teaspoon butter and 2 tablespoons goat cheese. Heat remaining 2 teaspoons butter in a large skillet over medium heat. Crack eggs into skillet; cook eggs until yolks are set, about 1 to 2 minutes per side. Sprinkle with salt and cayenne pepper to taste.

3. Drizzle each toast slice with about 2 tablespoons cayenne honey. Top each toast slice with a fried egg; drizzle evenly with remaining honey and sprinkle evenly with remaining cayenne chile. Serve.

Calories 610; **fat calories** 190; **total fat** 21g; **sat fat** 12g; **cholesterol** 225mg; **sodium** 510mg; **total carbohydrates** 86g; **fiber** 2g; **sugars** 44g; **protein** 19g; **vitamin A IUs** 20%; **vitamin C** 0%; **calcium** 10%; **iron** 20%

ROASTED POBLANO CHILE FRITTATA 🌶🌶

Poblano

FRESH

Frittatas are the perfect way to try fresh chile peppers—the eggs provide a perfect background for the flavors of each variety.

PREP TIME: **30 MIN.** / TOTAL TIME: **1 HR.** / SERVES: **6 (1 WEDGE)**

- 12 large eggs
- 3 fresh poblano chile peppers, roasted, peeled, stems and seeds removed, and diced
- 1 teaspoon dried oregano, crushed
- ¼ teaspoon salt
- ⅛ teaspoon freshly ground black pepper
- 1 tablespoon unsalted butter
- ½ small sweet onion, finely diced (about ¼ cup)
- 3 sun-dried tomatoes, finely diced (about 2 tablespoons)
- 2 garlic cloves, minced
- 8 ounces cream cheese, cubed

1. In a bowl, whisk together eggs, chile, oregano, salt, and black pepper.
2. In a large nonstick skillet, melt butter over medium-high heat. Add onion, tomato, and garlic; cook until onion is softened, stirring often, about 3 to 5 minutes. Stir in egg mixture; top with cream cheese. Cover and reduce heat to lowest setting; cook until eggs are set, about 20 minutes. Cut into 6 wedges. Serve.

Calories 250; **fat calories** 170; **total fat** 18g; **sat fat** 9g; **cholesterol** 355mg; **sodium** 200mg; **total carbohydrates** 10g; **fiber** 1g; **sugars** 4g; **protein** 12g; **vitamin A IUs** 30%; **vitamin C** 240%; **calcium** 8%; **iron** 10%

Heat It Up!
Spice up your morning by substituting fresh Cubanelle chile peppers for the poblanos.

BREAKFAST ENCHILADAS 〟

Serve this hearty dish with sour cream and chives to temper the heat.

PREP TIME: **45 MIN.** / TOTAL TIME: **1 HR. 35 MIN.** / SERVES: **5 (2 ENCHILADAS)**

Padron

FRESH

Red Fresno

FRESH

- 1 **pound baby Dutch yellow potatoes, halved lengthwise**
- 1 **pound fresh tomatillos, papery husks removed**
- 10 **fresh padron chile peppers (about 4 ounces), stems and seeds removed, halved**
- 2 **fresh red Fresno chile peppers, stems and seeds removed**
- 1 **large onion, quartered**
- 2 **tablespoons extra-virgin olive oil**

Salt

Freshly ground black pepper

- 1 **cup water**
- 2 **garlic cloves, peeled**
- ⅛ **teaspoon sugar**
- 1 **tablespoon unsalted butter**
- 6 **large eggs, beaten**
- 10 **6-inch corn tortillas**
- 2½ **cups shredded sharp cheddar cheese, divided (about 10 ounces)**

1. Preheat oven to 425°F. Line a baking sheet with foil. In a bowl, combine potato and next 5 ingredients (through oil); toss together; Sprinkle with salt and black pepper. Spread in a single layer on prepared baking sheet; roast at 425°F until charred, about 20 to 30 minutes. Cool slightly. Reduce oven temperature to 350°F.

2. Combine roasted tomatillo, onion, and Fresno chile with 1 cup water, garlic, and sugar in a blender*; process until smooth. Stir in salt and black pepper to taste. Transfer tomatillo mixture to shallow bowl.

3. In a nonstick skillet, melt butter over medium-high heat. Add eggs and scramble.

4. Dip each tortilla in tomatillo sauce; fill tortillas evenly with potato, padron chile, scrambled eggs, and cheese, using only 1¼ cups cheese. Roll filled tortillas as you prepare, arranging tightly, seam side down and side by side, in a 13 x 9–baking dish. Top enchiladas evenly with remaining tomatillo sauce and remaining 1¼ cups cheese. Bake at 350°F until cheese melts and enchiladas are heated through, about 20 minutes. Serve.

Note: *Be cautious when blending hot foods; the contents expand rapidly, causing a risk of scalding. To be safe, before blending, remove center piece of blender lid (to allow steam to escape), secure lid on blender, and place a towel over opening in lid (to avoid splatters).*

Calories 620; **fat calories** 330; **total fat** 37g; **sat fat** 16g; **cholesterol** 290mg; **sodium** 670mg; **total carbohydrates** 47g; **fiber** 8g; **sugars** 7g; **protein** 27g; **vitamin A IUs** 30%; **vitamin C** 110%; **calcium** 50%; **iron** 15%

Make Ahead

Assemble up to two days in advance and store in the baking dish, tightly covered, in the refrigerator. Let come to room temperature before baking.

De Arbol

DRIED

HOPPIN' TOAD IN THE HOLE 〃

If desired, garnish with chopped fresh parsley and serve with wedges of beefsteak tomato.

PREP TIME: **10 MIN.** / TOTAL TIME: **26 MIN**. / SERVES: **6 (1 BREAD SLICE)**

Cool It Down!
Turn down the heat by substituting dried Cascabel chile peppers for the de arbol chiles.

6   1-inch-thick slices sourdough bread, toasted
4   tablespoons unsalted butter (¼ cup)
2   dried de arbol chile peppers, stems and seeds removed, finely crushed
6   large eggs
½   cup shredded pepper-Jack cheese (about 2 ounces)
Salt
Freshly ground black pepper
Smoked paprika

1. Using a small round cookie cutter or juice glass, cut a 1½-inch hole in the center of each bread slice.

2. In a large skillet, melt 2 tablespoons butter over low heat; add half of crushed chile and cook until fragrant, stirring often, about 1 to 2 minutes. Increase heat to medium; arrange 3 bread slices in skillet. Crack 1 egg into the hole of each bread slice, taking care not to break yolks.

3. Cook until eggs are just firm but yolk is slightly runny, about 5 to 8 minutes. Sprinkle evenly with half of cheese during the last 2 minutes of cooking. Remove from skillet; keep warm. Repeat procedure with remaining butter, chile, bread slices, eggs, and cheese. Sprinkle bread slices with salt, black pepper, and paprika to taste. Serve.

Calories 360; **fat calories** 140; **total fat** 16g; **sat fat** 8g; **cholesterol** 215mg; **sodium** 460mg; **total carbohydrates** 38g; **fiber** 2g; **sugars** 2g; **protein** 16g; **vitamin A IUs** 15%; **vitamin C** 0%; **calcium** 10%; **iron** 20%

EGGS BENEDICT WITH RED FRESNO HOLLANDAISE ''

Red Fresno

FRESH

For a tasty variation, use smoked salmon slices instead of Canadian bacon.

PREP TIME: **25 MIN.** / TOTAL TIME: **50 MIN.** / SERVES: **8 (1 MUFFIN HALF)**

Hollandaise Sauce

- 16 tablespoons unsalted butter (1 cup)
- 3 large egg yolks
- 1 lemon, juiced (about 3 tablespoons)
- ¼ teaspoon salt
- ⅛ teaspoon freshly ground black pepper
- 2 fresh red Fresno chile peppers, stems and seeds removed, finely diced (about 3 tablespoons)

Poached Eggs

- 1 teaspoon salt
- 1 teaspoon white wine vinegar
- 8 large eggs

Remaining Ingredients

- 8 slices Canadian bacon (about 6 ounces)
- 4 English muffins, halved and toasted
- 1 tablespoon smoked paprika
- Freshly ground black pepper
- Fresh red Fresno chile peppers, thinly sliced

1. To make sauce, in a small saucepan, melt butter over low heat. In a glass bowl, combine egg yolks and next 4 ingredients (through chile), stirring with a whisk until smooth. Pour hot butter in a thin, steady stream into egg mixture while whisking vigorously until thickened, about 5 minutes. Whisk in additional salt and black pepper to taste.

2. To poach eggs, fill a large, straight-sided sauté pan with water to 1 inch from the top. Stir in 1 teaspoon salt and vinegar; bring to a simmer. Crack eggs, one at a time, into a small bowl or cup; gently lower into simmering water. After you drop the last egg, turn off heat; cover pan. Cook until egg whites are firm but yolk is runny, about 3 to 5 minutes. Transfer eggs with a slotted spoon to a paper towel–lined plate.

3. In large skillet, sear Canadian bacon over medium-high heat until browned, about 3 minutes per side. Top each muffin half with a piece of seared bacon and a poached egg; spoon hollandaise evenly over eggs. Sprinkle evenly with paprika, black pepper, and sliced chiles. Serve.

Calories 470; **fat calories** 280; **total fat** 32g; **sat fat** 17g; **cholesterol** 328mg; **sodium** 465mg; **total carbohydrates** 29g; **fiber** 1g; **sugars** 1g; **protein** 17g; **vitamin A IUs** 30%; **vitamin** C 30%; **calcium** 18%; **iron** 13%

Simple Swap

Homemade hollandaise sauce is preferable, but if you are short on time, use a packaged mix found in your local grocer.

Anaheim

FRESH

Make Ahead

Make and bake the quiches 5 minutes less; wrap well and freeze in an airtight container. To reheat, pop into a 350°F oven and bake until hot.

CHILE MINI QUICHES 🌶

These delightful little bites are perfect for brunch.

PREP TIME: **25 MIN.** / TOTAL TIME: **1 HR. 40 MIN.** / SERVES: **30 (1 MINI QUICHE)**

Pastry
- 1¼ cups all-purpose flour
- 1 tablespoon sugar
- ½ teaspoon salt
- 8 tablespoons cold unsalted butter, cut into 1-inch pieces (½ cup)
- 2 tablespoons cold water

Filling
- 3 large eggs
- 1 cup heavy cream
- ¼ pound Canadian bacon, finely chopped (about ½ cup)
- ¼ cup shredded smoked mozzarella cheese (about 2 ounces)
- ¼ cup shredded sharp cheddar cheese (about 2 ounces)
- ⅛ teaspoon salt
- ⅛ teaspoon freshly ground black pepper
- 3 fresh Anaheim chile peppers, roasted, peeled, stems and seeds removed, and diced (about ⅓ cup)
- 1 garlic clove, minced

1. To make pastry, place flour, sugar, and salt in a food processor; pulse 30 seconds. Add butter; process until mixture resembles coarse meal, about 15 seconds. With food processor on, pour 2 tablespoons water through feed tube in a slow, steady stream until dough just holds together when pinched. If necessary, add more water a few drops at a time. Do not process more than 30 seconds.
2. Turn dough out onto a clean work surface; gently form into a ball. Flatten ball into a disk and cover with plastic wrap; refrigerate at least 30 minutes.
3. Place chilled dough on a lightly floured surface; roll into a 13-inch round, rolling from the center outwards. (To ensure uniform thickness, lift up and turn pastry a quarter turn several times as you work.) Using a 2-inch cookie cutter, cut out dough and press rounds into cups of a nonstick mini muffin pan. Refrigerate, covered in plastic wrap, 30 minutes.
4. Preheat oven to 350°F. To make filling, in a bowl, whisk eggs vigorously until pale yellow in color and they flow in a steady stream when you lift the whisk, about 1 minute. Whisk in cream; stir in bacon and remaining ingredients.
5. Using a small ladle or measuring cup, pour filling into pastry cups. Bake at 350°F until eggs are set, about 15 minutes. Serve.

Calories 100; **fat calories** 60; **total fat** 7g; **sat fat** 4.5g; **cholesterol** 40mg; **sodium** 115mg; **total carbohydrates** 6g; **fiber** 0g; **sugars** 1g; **protein** 3g; **vitamin A IUs** 6%; **vitamin C** 60%; **calcium** 2%; **iron** 2%

QUINOA PATTIES WITH SUNNYSIDE-UP EGGS 🌶🌶

Quinoa, a high-protein grain-like seed that is considered a superfood, boasts high levels of fiber as well as iron, zinc, calcium, and other minerals. Its neutral flavor makes it a perfect supporting partner to the citrusy banana wax chile pepper.

PREP TIME: **20 MIN.** / TOTAL TIME: **55 MIN.** / SERVES: **8 (2 PATTIES & 1 EGG)**

1¼ cups red quinoa, cooked
1¼ cups white quinoa, cooked
12 large eggs, divided
 1 cup panko (Japanese breadcrumbs)
 ½ cup shredded pepper-Jack cheese (about 2 ounces)
 2 fresh banana wax chile peppers, stems and seeds removed, finely diced (about ⅔ cup)
 1 sweet onion, finely diced (about 1 cup)
 3 garlic cloves, minced
 ¼ teaspoon salt
 1 tablespoon extra-virgin olive oil

1. In a bowl, combine quinoas, 4 eggs, breadcrumbs, and next 5 ingredients (through salt). Form mixture into 16 patties.

2. Heat oil in a large skillet over medium-high heat. Add patties; cook until golden brown on both sides, turning once halfway through, about 10 to 12 minutes. Transfer to paper towels to drain. Into same skillet, crack remaining 8 eggs and lower heat. Cook until whites are set, about 5 minutes. Top 2 patties with 1 egg. Serve.

Calories 270; **fat calories** 110; **total fat** 12g; **sat fat** 4g; **cholesterol** 285mg; **sodium** 250mg; **total carbohydrates** 24g; **fiber** 3g; **sugars** 2g; **protein** 15g; **vitamin A IUs** 10%; **vitamin C** 35%; **calcium** 10%; **iron** 15%

CHERRY BELL AND EGG BREAKFAST SANDWICHES 🌶

The mild cherry bell chile pepper's fruity flavor is a reminder that peppers are, botanically, a type of berry.

PREP TIME: **15 MIN.** / TOTAL TIME: **30 MIN.** / SERVES: **4 (1 SANDWICH)**

4   slices bacon, halved
4   fresh cherry bell chile peppers, stems and seeds removed, cut into ¼-inch rings
4   large eggs
1   teaspoon smoked paprika
Salt
Freshly ground black pepper
4   slices Gruyère cheese
2   tablespoons mayonnaise
8   slices egg bread (lightly toasted, if desired)
8   thin slices beefsteak tomato (1 large tomato)
4   leaves romaine lettuce

1. Heat a large skillet over medium-high heat. Add bacon; cook until crisp, about 3 to 5 minutes per side. Transfer to paper towels to drain.

2. Add chile rings to hot bacon grease in skillet; cook over medium-high heat until cooked through but still crisp, about 3 to 5 minutes. Transfer chile rings to paper towels to drain. Discard all but 1 table-spoon bacon grease from skillet.

3. Add eggs to skillet; fry until whites are set, about 2 minutes; flip eggs and flatten slightly to break yolks. Sprinkle evenly with paprika; sprinkle with salt and black pepper to taste. Top each egg evenly with bell pepper rings and 1 slice cheese; cook until eggs are set and cheese is melted, about 2 minutes.

4. Spread mayonnaise evenly on 4 bread slices; top evenly with tomato slices, lettuce, bacon, and prepared eggs. Top with remaining bread slices. Serve.

Calories 540; **fat calories** 250; **total fat** 28g; **sat fat** 10g; **cholesterol** 270mg; **sodium** 650mg; **total carbohydrates** 45g; **fiber** 4g; **sugars** 5g; **protein** 27g; **vitamin A IUs** 80%; **vitamin C** 90%; **calcium** 40%; **iron** 25%

MEXICAN O'BRIEN POTATOES

This classic breakfast side is rumored to have been created by a New York City restaurant in the early 1900s.

Bell Pepper

FRESH

PREP TIME: **30 MIN.** / TOTAL TIME: **50 MIN.** / SERVES: **6 (ABOUT 1 CUP)**

- 3 tablespoons extra-virgin olive oil
- ½ pound Dutch yellow potatoes, finely diced (about 1½ cups)
- ½ pound ruby gold potatoes, finely diced (about 1½ cups)
- 1 small fresh green bell pepper, stem and seeds removed, diced (about ½ cup)
- 1 small fresh red bell pepper, stem and seeds removed, diced (about ½ cup)
- 1 sweet onion, diced

Salt

Freshly ground black pepper

- 2 teaspoons smoked paprika
- 1 cup shredded pepper-Jack cheese (about 4 ounces)

1. Heat oil in a large skillet over medium heat. Add potatoes, bell peppers, and onion; cook until potato is tender, stirring occasionally, about 15 minutes. Sprinkle with salt and black pepper to taste. Sprinkle with paprika and cheese; let sit until cheese is melted. Serve.

Calories 220; **fat calories** 140; **total fat** 15g; **sat fat** 5g; **cholesterol** 15mg; **sodium** 320mg; **total carbohydrates** 17g; **fiber** 3g; **sugars** 2g; **protein** 6g; **vitamin A IUs** 15%; **vitamin C** 60%; **calcium** 15%; **iron** 6%

Cubanelle

FRESH

BACON AND EGG-STUFFED CUBANELLE CHILES 🌶

Cubanelle chile peppers are available fresh in red or green varieties; choose one color or mix it up with a combination.

PREP TIME: **20 MIN.** / TOTAL TIME: **1 HR.** / SERVES: **8 (1 STUFFED CHILE)**

8 large fresh Cubanelle chile peppers (about 1½ pounds), roasted and peeled
6 slices thick-cut bacon, diced (about ½ pound)
5 tablespoons unsalted butter, divided
10 large eggs, beaten
⅓ cup sun-dried tomatoes, chopped
Salt
Freshly ground black pepper
3 tablespoons all-purpose flour
2 cups whole milk
1 cup shredded pepper-Jack cheese (about 4 ounces)

1. Make a lengthwise cut along the side of each chile and carefully remove seeds, leaving stem on and keeping peppers intact.
2. Preheat oven to 350°F. Line a baking sheet with foil. Heat a large skillet over medium-high heat. Add bacon; cook until crisp, about 10 minutes. Transfer to paper towels to drain. Discard all but about 1 tablespoon bacon grease from skillet. Add 2 tablespoons butter to skillet; melt over medium-low heat. Add eggs; scramble just until fluffy, about 3 to 5 minutes. Add bacon and tomato; sprinkle with salt and black pepper to taste. Cool egg mixture slightly.
3. Spoon egg mixture evenly into chiles; arrange on prepared baking sheet. Bake at 350°F until heated through, about 10 minutes.
4. Melt remaining 3 tablespoons butter in a medium saucepan. Add flour; cook until golden brown and smooth, stirring constantly, about 3 to 5 minutes. Slowly stir in milk. Reduce heat; simmer until sauce coats the back of a spoon, about 5 minutes. Remove from heat; add cheese, stirring until melted and smooth. Drizzle stuffed chiles evenly with cheese sauce. Serve.

Calories 430; **fat calories** 280; **total fat** 31g; **sat fat** 14g; **cholesterol** 295mg; **sodium** 820mg; **total carbohydrates** 14g; **fiber** 1g; **sugars** 7g; **protein** 24g; **vitamin A IUs** 35%; **vitamin C** 300%; **calcium** 20%; **iron** 10%

FARRO, CHILE, AND MUSHROOM PATTIES 🌶

Cubanelle

FRESH

Wheat berries are a good substitute if farro is unavailable. Serve these patties alongside a colorful fruit salad.

PREP TIME: **50 MIN.** / TOTAL TIME: **2 HR.** / SERVES: **10 (1 PATTY)**

1   6-ounce package organic farro
1   pound Dutch yellow potatoes, halved
4   tablespoons extra-virgin olive oil, divided
4   tablespoons unsalted butter, divided (¼ cup)
2   sweet onions, thinly sliced
1   pound fresh button mushrooms, chopped
1   tablespoon smoked paprika
1   tablespoon dried Italian seasoning, crushed
½   teaspoon salt
½   teaspoon freshly ground black pepper
3   garlic cloves, minced
2   fresh Cubanelle chile peppers, stems and seeds removed, chopped
2   tablespoons dry sherry
1   cup panko (Japanese breadcrumbs)
1   cup shredded Gruyère cheese (about 8 ounces)
¼   cup fresh chives, finely chopped (about 24 whole chives)
2   large eggs
⅓   cup canola oil

1. Prepare farro according to package directions. Place potatoes in a medium saucepan with enough cold water to cover. Cook until fork tender, about 15 minutes. Drain; transfer to a large bowl and mash.

2. Heat 2 tablespoons olive oil and 2 tablespoons butter in a large skillet over medium-high heat. Add onion; cook until softened and browned, stirring occasionally, about 5 to 7 minutes. Add onion to potato.

3. Heat remaining 2 tablespoons olive oil and remaining 2 tablespoons butter in skillet over medium-high heat. Add mushrooms and next 6 ingredients (through chiles); cook until mushrooms are soft, stirring occasionally, about 5 to 7 minutes. Stir in sherry. Reduce heat; simmer until most of the mushroom liquid is reduced, about 5 minutes.

4. Add mushroom mixture, breadcrumbs, cheese, chives, and eggs to potato mixture; stir to combine. Fold farro into potato mixture until well combined. Form farro mixture into 10 patties, each about ¼ inch thick.

5. Heat canola oil in skillet over medium-high heat. Fry patties until golden brown, about 5 minutes per side. Serve.

Calories 330; **fat calories** 160; **total fat** 18g; **sat fat** 6g; **cholesterol** 60mg; **sodium** 240mg; **total carbohydrates** 33g; **fiber** 5g; **sugars** 5g; **protein** 11g; **vitamin A IUs** 20%; **vitamin C** 35%; **calcium** 15%; **iron** 10%

Make Ahead

Freeze any leftover cooked patties between layers of butcher paper or wax paper. They will keep, tightly sealed and frozen, for up to one month.

POACHED EGGS OVER SAUSAGE 🌶🌶🌶

Habanero

DRIED

Hot, lively habanero chile peppers rev up this breakfast. Serve with a stack of warmed corn tortillas and small roasted potatoes.

PREP TIME: **25 MIN.** / TOTAL TIME: **1 HR. 50 MIN.** / SERVES: **4 (2 PATTIES & 2 EGGS)**

1	dried habanero chile pepper
½	pound ground sweet Italian sausage
½	pound ground spicy Italian sausage
1	pound tomatillos, papery husks removed
4	teaspoons olive oil, divided
1	sweet onion, diced (about 1 cup)
2	garlic cloves, minced
2	cups chicken broth
1	teaspoon salt
1	tablespoon white wine vinegar
8	large eggs

1. In a bowl, combine chile and cold water to cover until reconstituted, about 30 minutes. Drain.

2. In a bowl, combine sausages and form into 8 patties. Cover and chill until using.

3. Preheat broiler to high. Line a baking sheet with foil. In a bowl, combine tomatillos with 2 teaspoons oil; toss together. Arrange in a single layer on baking sheet. Broil, about 4 inches from heat, until tomatillos blister, blacken, and soften, turning as needed, about 10 to 12 minutes. Place tomatillos and chile in a food processor or blender*; process until smooth.

4. Heat remaining 2 teaspoons oil in a large saucepan over medium heat. Add onion and garlic; cook until deep golden brown, stirring often, about 7 to 10 minutes. Increase heat to high; add tomatillo mixture. Cook until mixture just boils, stirring often, about 4 to 5 minutes. Add broth; return to a boil. Reduce heat; simmer until slightly reduced, about 10 minutes.

5. Heat a large skillet over medium-high heat. Add sausage patties; cook until browned and cooked completely through, turning once halfway through, about 10 to 12 minutes. Keep warm.

6. Fill a large, straight-sided sauté pan with water to 1 inch from the top. Stir in salt and vinegar; bring to a simmer. Crack 2 or 3 eggs, one at a time, into a small bowl or cup; gently lower into simmering water. After you drop the last egg, turn off heat; cover pan. Cook until egg whites are firm but yolks are runny, about 3 to 5 minutes. Remove poached eggs with a slotted spoon; transfer to a paper towel–lined plate. Repeat to poach all the eggs.

7. Top each sausage patty with an egg; top evenly with tomatillo mixture. Serve.

Note: *Be cautious when blending hot foods; the contents expand rapidly, causing a risk of scalding. To be safe, before blending, remove center piece of blender lid (to allow steam to escape), secure lid on blender, and place a towel over opening in lid (to avoid splatters).*

Calories 530; **fat calories** 330; **total fat** 37g; **sat fat** 12g; **cholesterol** 425mg; **sodium** 1,430mg; **total carbohydrates** 19g; **fiber** 4g; **sugars** 8g; **protein** 30g; **vitamin A IUs** 20%; **vitamin C** 30%; **calcium** 10%; **iron** 20%

FIERY FRENCH TOAST 🌶

Shishito

Shishito chile peppers can be hit and miss on the heat scale, ranging from mild to spicy. Each bite will be a mystery!

PREP TIME: **15 MIN.** / TOTAL TIME: **35 MIN.** / SERVES: **8 (1 SLICE TOAST)**

⅔ cup whole milk

1½ teaspoons pure vanilla extract

⅛ teaspoon sugar

6 large eggs

10 fresh shishito chile peppers, stems and seeds removed, chopped, divided (about 2 ounces)

8 slices buttermilk bread

4 tablespoons unsalted butter, softened (¼ cup)

¾ cup maple syrup

1. In a shallow bowl, whisk together milk, vanilla, sugar, and eggs. Stir in half of shishito chile.

2. Heat a large nonstick skillet over medium heat. Dip bread in egg mixture; place in hot skillet. Cook until golden brown, about 4 minutes per side. Spread softened butter evenly on one side of each slice.

3. In a small saucepan, combine remaining half of shishito chiles and syrup. Bring to a simmer over medium-high heat; immediately remove from heat. Drizzle syrup evenly over bread slices. Serve.

Calories 315; **fat calories** 105; **total fat** 12g; **sat fat** 6g; **cholesterol** 160mg; **sodium** 285mg; **total carbohydrates** 45g; **fiber** 1g; **sugars** 27g; **protein** 11g; **vitamin A IUs** 10%; **vitamin C** 15%; **calcium** 23%; **iron** 10%

Simple Swap

If you can't find buttermilk bread, substitute home-style white bread.

GUAJILLO CHILE ZUCCHINI BREAD 〃

We guarantee this zucchini bread will be a hit at your next brunch. Make a double batch to have extra on hand after the first loaf disappears.

PREP TIME: **30 MIN.** / TOTAL TIME: **1 HR. 50 MIN.** / SERVES: **12 (2 SLICES)**

Guajillo

DRIED

- 3 cups all-purpose flour
- 1 tablespoon ground cinnamon
- 1 teaspoon salt
- 1 teaspoon baking powder
- 1 teaspoon baking soda
- 6 dried guajillo chile peppers, stems and seeds removed, ground
- 3 large eggs
- 1 cup canola oil
- 1 teaspoon pure vanilla extract
- 2¼ cups sugar
- 2 cups grated zucchini (about 1 large)
- 2 lemons, zested
- ¾ cup red walnut pieces

1. Preheat oven to 325°F. Lightly spray 2 (8 x 4–inch) loaf pans with cooking spray. Line bottoms of pans with parchment paper; lightly spray parchment paper with cooking spray. In a bowl, sift together flour, cinnamon, salt, baking powder, and baking soda. Stir in chile.

2. In the bowl of a mixer fitted with a whisk, beat eggs, oil, vanilla, and sugar on medium speed until mixture is smooth and off-white in color, about 3 minutes. With mixer on low, slowly add flour mixture, mixing until smooth and well combined.

3. Remove whisk and attach a paddle to the mixer. Add zucchini, zest, and walnuts to egg-flour mixture; mix thoroughly. Pour equal amounts of batter into prepared pans. Bake at 325°F until a toothpick inserted into center comes out clean, about 60 to 75 minutes. Cool on wire rack, in pans, 10 minutes. Remove loaves from pans and remove parchment paper; cool completely on wire rack. Cut into 24 slices. Serve.

Calories 270; **fat calories** 110; **total fat** 12g; **sat fat** 1g; **cholesterol** 25mg; **sodium** 180mg; **total carbohydrates** 37g; **fiber** 1g; **sugars** 20g; **protein** 3g; **vitamin A IUs** 15%; **vitamin C** 4%; **calcium** 2%; **iron** 4%

Kitchen Savvy

Be sure to squeeze the grated zucchini between towels to remove extra moisture.

soups
and salads

» **ROASTED BUTTERNUT SQUASH SOUP**

71

Red Fresno

FRESH

ROASTED BUTTERNUT SQUASH SOUP ""

For an attractive—and tasty—presentation, garnish the finished soup with sliced chiles and chives in addition to the crispy pancetta.

PREP TIME: **35 MIN.** / TOTAL TIME: **1 HR. 30 MIN.** / SERVES: **6 (ABOUT 2 CUPS)**

1 butternut squash, peeled, seeded, and cut into 1-inch cubes (about 2 pounds)
5 tablespoons extra-virgin olive oil, divided
Salt
Freshly ground black pepper
6 ounces pancetta, diced, divided (about 1 cup)
3 fresh red Fresno chile peppers, stems and seeds removed, 2 chopped, 1 sliced
2 garlic cloves, minced
1 large onion, chopped (about 1 cup)
2½ cups chicken broth
1 14.5-ounce can diced tomatoes, undrained
2 tablespoons dry sherry

1. Preheat oven to 425°F. Line a baking sheet with foil. In a large bowl, toss squash cubes with 3 tablespoons olive oil, ½ teaspoon salt, and ¼ teaspoon black pepper. Arrange squash in a single layer on baking sheet. Bake at 425°F until tender, about 20 minutes.
2. Heat remaining 2 tablespoons oil in a Dutch oven over medium-high heat. Add one-third of pancetta; cook until browned, stirring occasionally, about 7 minutes. Transfer to a plate to drain. Add chopped chile, garlic, and onion to hot oil in Dutch oven; cook 5 minutes. Add remaining two-thirds pancetta; cook, stirring often, 3 minutes.
3. Add roasted squash, broth, tomatoes, and sherry; bring just to boiling. Reduce heat to low; simmer until tomatoes start to break apart, about 5 minutes. Cover; simmer 15 minutes. Place squash mixture in a blender*; process until smooth. Stir in salt and black pepper to taste. Top evenly with pancetta. Serve.

*Note: Be cautious when blending hot foods; the contents expand rapidly, causing a risk of scalding. To be safe, before blending, remove center piece of blender lid (to allow steam to escape), secure lid on blender, and place a towel over opening in lid (to avoid splatters).

Calories 300; **fat calories** 170; **total fat** 20g; **sat fat** 4.5g; **cholesterol** 20mg; **sodium** 740mg; **total carbohydrates** 25g; **fiber** 6g; **sugars** 9g; **protein** 8g; **vitamin A IUs** 290%; **vitamin C** 80%; **calcium** 8%; **iron** 8%

FRESH SCALLOP AND GRILLED CORN CHOWDER 🌶🌶🌶

Thai

FRESH

This recipe uses bay scallops, which are about the size of small grapes.

PREP TIME: **25 MIN.** / TOTAL TIME: **1 HR. 20 MIN.** / SERVES: **15 (ABOUT 1½ CUPS)**

- 4 ears fresh corn, husked and cleaned
- ½ pound bacon, finely diced
- 1 pound fresh Bay scallops, rinsed and drained
- 8 garlic cloves, minced
- 4 fresh Thai chile peppers, stems and seeds removed
- 2 ribs celery, finely diced (about ⅔ cup)
- 1 onion, finely diced (about 1 cup)
- 8 tablespoons unsalted butter (½ cup)
- 1 cup all-purpose flour
- 5 cups whole milk
- 2 cups heavy cream
- 2 bay leaves
- 2 large Yukon Gold potatoes, peeled and cut into ½-inch pieces (about 3 cups)

Salt
Freshly ground black pepper

1. Preheat grill to medium-high. Place corn on grill rack; grill until slightly charred, about 10 minutes. Cool until can be handled, about 15 minutes. Carefully cut kernels from cobs.

2. Heat a large saucepan over medium heat. Add bacon; cook until crisp, about 7 to 10 minutes. Add scallops; cook just until lightly browned, about 3 to 5 minutes.

Remove scallops from saucepan.

3. Add garlic, chile, celery, and onion to saucepan; cook until onion is softened, stirring constantly, about 5 minutes. Add butter; cook, until melted, stirring constantly. Add flour; cook until golden brown, stirring constantly, about 3 minutes. Slowly whisk in milk and cream. Add bay leaves and potato; bring just to boiling. Reduce heat to low and cover; simmer until potato is tender, about 15 minutes.

4. Remove bay leaves; stir in scallops and corn. Simmer until corn and scallops are just cooked through, about 5 to 7 minutes. Stir in salt and black pepper to taste. Serve.

Calories 405; **fat calories** 247; **total fat** 27g; **sat fat** 15g; **cholesterol** 87mg; **sodium** 400mg; **total carbohydrates** 31g; **fiber** 2g; **sugars** 8g; **protein** 13g; **vitamin A IUs** 17%; **vitamin C** 20%; **calcium** 13%; **iron** 7%

Simple Swap

Fresh corn not in season? No problem. Stir in 3 cups of frozen corn when you add the scallops in step 4.

KICKIN' CRAB AND GRILLED CORN CHOWDER)))

This big batch of soup can easily be halved for smaller groups.

PREP TIME: **30 MIN.** / TOTAL TIME: **1 HR. 45 MIN.** / SERVES: **12 (ABOUT 2 CUPS)**

8 tablespoons unsalted butter, divided (½ cup)
4 ears fresh corn, husked and cleaned
Salt
Freshly ground black pepper
½ pound bacon, finely chopped
10 to 12 finely chopped shallots (about ½ cup)
8 garlic cloves, minced
2 ribs celery, trimmed and finely chopped (about ¾ cup)
2 dried japones chile peppers, stems and seeds removed
1 sweet onion, diced (about ⅔ cup)
½ cup all-purpose flour
6 cups whole milk
2 cups heavy cream
2 bay leaves
2 large Yukon Gold potatoes, peeled and cut into ½-inch pieces (about 3 cups)
1 pound fresh crabmeat, cleaned
Chopped fresh parsley
Ground dried japones chiles (optional)

1. Heat grill to medium-high heat. Melt 4 tablespoons butter; brush evenly on corn. Sprinkle with salt and black pepper. Place corn on grill rack; grill until slightly charred, about 10 minutes.

Carefully cut kernels from cobs.
2. Heat a large saucepan over medium heat. Add bacon; cook until crisp, about 3 to 5 minutes. Add shallots and next 4 ingredients (through sweet onion); cook until onion is translucent, about 5 minutes. Stir in remaining 4 tablespoons butter; cook until butter melts.
3. Add flour; cook until smooth, stirring constantly, about 3 minutes. Slowly whisk in milk and cream. Add bay leaves and potato; bring just to boiling. Reduce heat to low and cover; simmer until potato is tender, about 15 minutes.
4. Remove bay leaves; stir in crabmeat and corn. Simmer until crabmeat and corn are thoroughly heated through, about 10 minutes. Stir in salt and black pepper to taste; sprinkle with parsley and ground chile, if desired. Serve.

Calories 540; **fat calories** 320; **total fat** 35g; **sat fat** 19g; **cholesterol** 135mg; **sodium** 510mg; **total carbohydrates** 39g; **fiber** 3g; **sugars** 12g; **protein** 22g; **vitamin A IUs** 20%; **vitamin C** 20%; **calcium** 25%; **iron** 8%

Japones

DRIED

Kitchen Savvy
A corn zipper can help remove the kernels from the cob more quickly and safely than a knife.

BEER, CHEESE, AND SAVINA CHILE SOUP))))

This rich soup can be made with light or dark beer, and is thick enough to qualify as a fondue.

PREP TIME: **40 MIN.** / TOTAL TIME: **1 HR. 10 MIN.** / SERVES: **10 (ABOUT 1½ CUPS)**

Heat It Up!

Add extra chopped red Savina habanero chile to your soup for a powerful punch.

2 tablespoons extra-virgin olive oil
6 veggie sweet mini peppers, stems and seeds removed, chopped (about ⅔ cup)
2 carrots, peeled and chopped
2 ribs celery, trimmed and chopped
1 small sweet onion, finely chopped (about ⅔ cup)
2 garlic cloves, minced
1 fresh red Savina habanero chile pepper, stem and seeds removed, halved
3 cups chicken broth
2 cups beer
⅓ cup unsalted butter
⅓ cup all-purpose flour
4 cups whole milk
6 cups shredded sharp cheddar cheese (about 1½ pounds)
Salt
Fresh chopped chives

1. Heat oil in a medium saucepan over medium-high heat. Add mini pepper, carrot, celery, and onion; cook until just softened, about 5 minutes. Add garlic and chile; cook 1 minute. Stir in broth and beer; bring just to boiling. Reduce heat; simmer 15 minutes.
2. Melt butter in a Dutch oven; stir in flour. Cook until flour mixture turns golden brown (blonde roux), stirring constantly, about 5 minutes. Slowly stir in milk; stir in cheese until melted.
3. Place half of beer-vegetable mixture in a blender*; process until smooth. Stir blended mixture into cheese mixture; stir in remaining beer-vegetable mixture. Stir in salt to taste; sprinkle with chopped chives. Serve.

***Note:** Be cautious when blending hot foods; the contents expand rapidly, causing a risk of scalding. To be safe, before blending, remove center piece of blender lid (to allow steam to escape), secure lid on blender, and place a towel over opening in lid (to avoid splatters).*

Calories 485; **fat calories** 322; **total fat** 35g; **sat fat** 20g; **cholesterol** 96mg; **sodium** 626mg; **total carbohydrates** 17g; **fiber** 2g; **sugars** 8g; **protein** 22g; **vitamin A IUs** 141%; **vitamin C** 39%; **calcium** 60%; **iron** 5%

HEIRLOOM TOMATO AND PIQUILLO PEPPER SOUP

Serve with a spoonful of plain yogurt or sour cream and a sprinkle of small fresh basil leaves, if desired.

PREP TIME: **30 MIN.** / TOTAL TIME: **1 HR. 20 MIN.** / SERVES: **8 (ABOUT 1¾ CUPS)**

6   garlic cloves, peeled
3   pounds fresh heirloom tomatoes
2   sweet onions, peeled and quartered
¼   cup extra-virgin olive oil
½   teaspoon salt
¼   teaspoon freshly ground white pepper
4   cups chicken broth
6   jarred piquillo chile peppers, chopped (about ⅓ cup)
6   dried California chile peppers, stems and seeds removed (about 3 ounces)
4   tablespoons unsalted butter (¼ cup)
1   cup fresh basil leaves

1. Preheat oven to 425°F. Line a baking sheet with foil. In a bowl, combine garlic, tomatoes, and onion; add oil, salt, and white pepper; toss to coat. Arrange in a single layer on prepared baking sheet; roast at 425°F until tomatoes are softened, stirring occasionally, about 30 minutes.

2. In a large saucepan, combine roasted vegetables, broth, piquillo pepper, and California chiles; bring just to boiling. Reduce heat; simmer 20 minutes. Remove from heat; remove California chiles.

Stir in butter and basil. Place half of vegetable mixture in a blender*; process until smooth. Add back to vegetable mixture in saucepan. Serve.

*Note: Be cautious when blending hot foods; the contents expand rapidly, causing a risk of scalding. To be safe, before blending, remove center piece of blender lid (to allow steam to escape), secure lid on blender, and place a towel over opening in lid (to avoid splatters).

Calories 338; **fat calories** 113; **total fat** 13g; **sat fat** 5g; **cholesterol** 15mg; **sodium** 278 mg; **total carbohydrates** 53g; **fiber** 3g; **sugars** 8g; **protein** 3g; **vitamin A IUs** 110%; **vitamin C** 80%; **calcium** 8%; **iron** 6%

Poblano

FRESH

ALBONDIGAS SOUP ❯

This now-traditionally Mexican soup originated in Moorish Spain: "Albondigas" is derived from the Arabic word for hazelnuts, referencing the small size of the meatballs.

PREP TIME: **40 MIN.** / TOTAL TIME: **1 HR. 30 MIN.** / SERVES: **10 (ABOUT 2 CUPS)**

Make Ahead

Brown the meatballs up to 2 days ahead of time. When finishing the soup, increase the simmer time from 10 to 20 minutes.

1	pound ground beef
2	onions, finely chopped, divided
½	cup dry Italian breadcrumbs
¼	cup grated Parmesan cheese (about 1 ounce)
½	teaspoon salt
½	teaspoon freshly ground black pepper
2	garlic cloves, minced
	Cold water
2	tablespoons extra-virgin olive oil
3	quarts beef broth
1	28-ounce can whole tomatoes, undrained
1¼	pounds fresh poblano chile peppers, roasted, peeled, stems and seeds removed, and chopped (about 4 large)
1½	teaspoons dried basil, crushed
1½	teaspoons dried oregano, crushed
1	teaspoon Tabasco sauce
½	cup quick-cooking long grain rice
½	cup chopped fresh cilantro

1. In a bowl, combine beef, half of onion, breadcrumbs, and next 4 ingredients (through garlic). Add a little cold water as you combine, keeping beef mixture moist but not wet. Form beef mixture into small balls.

2. Heat oil in a large skillet over medium-high heat. Add meatballs; cook until browned, turning often, about 12 to 15 minutes.

3. In a large saucepan, combine broth and tomatoes; stir in remaining half of onion, chile, basil, oregano, and Tabasco sauce. Bring just to boiling. Stir in rice. Reduce heat and cover; simmer 15 minutes.

4. Add meatballs and cover; simmer until meatballs and rice are fully cooked, about 10 minutes. Stir in cilantro; stir in additional salt and black pepper, if desired. Serve.

Calories 260; **fat calories** 100; **total fat** 11g; **sat fat** 4g; **cholesterol** 35mg; **sodium** 1,020mg; **total carbohydrates** 25g; **fiber** 2g; **sugars** 8g; **protein** 15g; **vitamin A IUs** 20%; **vitamin C** 260%; **calcium** 10%; **iron** 20%

Pequin

BANANA SQUASH AND CHILE SOUP 🌶🌶

Banana squash grow to at least three feet long and usually are sold in pieces. Feel free to substitute an equal amount of any winter squash.

PREP TIME: **30 MIN.** / TOTAL TIME: **1 HR. 40 MIN.** / SERVES: **6 (ABOUT 2 CUPS)**

Cool It Down!
To keep some of the heat but not all of the fire, try dried de arbol chile peppers instead.

3½ pounds banana squash, peeled and cut into chunks

3 tablespoons extra-virgin olive oil, divided

¼ teaspoon salt

2 tablespoons unsalted butter

1 sweet onion, chopped (about 1 cup)

15 dried pequin chile peppers, crushed (about 2 teaspoons)

2 garlic cloves, chopped

1 28-ounce can whole peeled tomatoes, undrained

1 cup white wine

4 cups chicken broth

¼ cup sherry

1. Preheat oven to 350°F. Line a baking sheet with foil. In a bowl, toss squash with 1 tablespoon oil. Arrange in an even layer on prepared baking sheet; sprinkle evenly with salt. Bake at 350°F until almost tender, about 20 minutes. Cool squash until can be handled, about 10 minutes; chop.

2. Heat remaining 2 tablespoons oil and butter in a large saucepan over medium-high heat. Add onion and chile; cook until onion is softened, about 3 minutes. Add garlic; cook until fragrant, about 30 seconds. Stir in tomatoes; crush tomatoes with a fork. Stir in wine; bring just to boiling. Reduce heat; simmer 7 minutes.

3. Stir in squash, broth, and sherry. Return to a boil; cook 3 minutes. Reduce heat to medium-low and cover; simmer until squash is tender, about 30 minutes. Remove from heat; let stand 10 minutes. Place squash mixture in a blender*; process until smooth. Serve.

*Note: Be cautious when blending hot foods; the contents expand rapidly, causing a risk of scalding. To be safe, before blending, remove center piece of blender lid (to allow steam to escape), secure lid on blender, and place a towel over opening in lid (to avoid splatters).

Calories 260; **fat calories** 70; **total fat** 8g; **sat fat** 3g; **cholesterol** 10mg; **sodium** 650mg; **total carbohydrates** 34g; **fiber** 4g; **sugars** 14g; **protein** 5g; **vitamin A IUs** 240%; **vitamin C** 80%; **calcium** 8%; **iron** 10%

BEEF TORTILLA SOUP 〟

For an extra note of authenticity, try this recipe with goat meat instead of beef and add sprigs of fresh cilantro as a garnish. You can usually purchase goat meat at Mexican or Middle Eastern supermarkets.

PREP TIME: **30 MIN.** / TOTAL TIME: **3 HR.** / SERVES: **12 (ABOUT 2 CUPS)**

- 2 pounds stew meat (such as beef chuck), cut into 1-inch pieces
- ½ teaspoon salt
- ¼ teaspoon black pepper
- 1 28-ounce can red chili sauce
- 3 tablespoons extra-virgin olive oil
- 1 large sweet onion, finely chopped (about 1¼ cups)
- 4 garlic cloves, minced
- 2 carrots, peeled and finely chopped (about 1 cup)
- 2 ribs celery, chopped (about ¾ cup)
- 5 cups beef broth
- 1 28-ounce can stewed tomatoes, undrained
- 2 dried Hatch chile peppers, stems and seeds removed
- 1 large fresh green bell pepper, stem and seeds removed, finely chopped
- 1 3-ounce package dried sweet corn or 1 cup frozen sweet corn kernels
- 1 dried California chile, stem and seeds removed, ground
- 1 teaspoon dried oregano, crushed
- 1 teaspoon ground cumin
- 1 avocado, diced

Tortilla chips (optional)
Shredded Monterey Jack cheese (optional)

1. Sprinkle beef evenly with salt and black pepper. In a large saucepan, combine beef and chili sauce over medium-high heat; bring chili sauce just to bubbling. Reduce heat and partially cover; simmer until meat is tender, stirring often, about 1½ to 2 hours.

2. Heat oil in a large saucepan over medium-high heat. Add onion; cook until browned, stirring occasionally, about 7 minutes. Add garlic, carrot, and celery; cook 3 minutes. Add beef, chili sauce, broth, tomatoes, Hatch chile, bell pepper, corn, California chile, oregano, and cumin. Bring just to boiling. Reduce heat and partially cover; simmer until liquid is slightly reduced, stirring occasionally, about 30 minutes.

3. Top with avocado; top with tortilla chips and cheese, if desired. Serve.

Calories 370; **fat calories** 160; **total fat** 18g; **sat fat** 5g; **cholesterol** 40 mg; **sodium** 875mg; **total carbohydrates** 35g; **fiber** 6g; **sugars** 6g; **protein** 19g; **vitamin A IUs** 100%; **vitamin C** 30%; **calcium** 5%; **iron** 15%

Hatch

DRIED

Bell Pepper

FRESH

California

DRIED

Manzano

FRESH

TOMATO, CUCUMBER, AND GRILLED CORN SALAD 🌶

Heirloom tomatoes come in a wide variety of shapes, sizes, and colors and boast a deep, rich tomato flavor that speaks of summer. If you can't find baby heirlooms, use gold teardrop or grape tomatoes.

PREP TIME: **30 MIN.** / TOTAL TIME: **1 HR. 10 MIN.** / SERVES: **6 (ABOUT 1½ CUPS)**

Heat It Up!

Fire up the flavor by using fresh red Savina habanero chile peppers in place of the manzano chile peppers.

2 fresh manzano chile peppers
Extra-virgin olive oil
4 ears fresh sweet corn, husked and cleaned
2 pounds baby heirloom tomatoes, halved
½ cup loosely packed fresh basil, chopped
¼ cup balsamic vinegar
4 baby cucumbers, sliced (about ¾ pound)
3 garlic cloves, minced
Salt

1. Preheat grill to medium-high. Rub chiles with oil. Place corn and chiles on grill rack; grill until slightly charred, about 10 minutes. Cool until can be handled, about 15 minutes. Carefully cut kernels from cobs. Peel chiles and remove stems and seeds; chop chiles.

2. In a large bowl, combine corn, chile, tomato, and next 4 ingredients (through garlic); toss together. Sprinkle with salt to taste. Serve.

Calories 90; **fat calories** 10; **total fat** 1g; **sat fat** 0g; **cholesterol** 0mg; **sodium** 410mg; **total carbohydrates** 19g; **fiber** 4g; **sugars** 7g; **protein** 4g; **vitamin A IUs** 30%; **vitamin C** 60%; **calcium** 2%; **iron** 4%

SPICY CUCUMBER AND RADISH SALAD 🌶🌶🌶

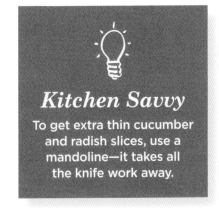

Scorpion

FRESH

The scorpion chile pepper is one of the hottest in the world, hotter even than the bhut jolokia (ghost) pepper. This recipe starts out with just a quarter of a pepper. For those feeling bolder, try a half—but have some extra plain yogurt on hand to put out that fire.

PREP TIME: **20 MIN.** / TOTAL TIME: **50 MIN.** / SERVES: **4 (ABOUT ¾ CUP)**

¼ cup sour cream

¼ cup nonfat Greek yogurt

¼ cup fresh cilantro, finely chopped

2 tablespoons seasoned rice vinegar

¼ teaspoon granulated sugar

¼ fresh scorpion chile pepper, stem and seeds removed, finely diced

6 mini cucumbers, sliced ⅛ inch thick (about 1 pound)

6 red radishes, sliced ⅛ inch thick

Salt

1. In a bowl, whisk together sour cream and next 5 ingredients (through chile). In a large bowl, combine cucumber and radish. Stir in sour cream mixture and salt to taste. Refrigerate, covered, 30 minutes. Serve.

Calories 70; **fat calories** 35; **total fat** 4g; **sat fat** 3g; **cholesterol** 10mg; **sodium** 140mg; **total carbohydrates** 6g; **fiber** 2g; **sugars** 4g; **protein** 3g; **vitamin A IUs** 80%; **vitamin C** 20%; **calcium** 4%; **iron** 0%

Kitchen Savvy

To get extra thin cucumber and radish slices, use a mandoline—it takes all the knife work away.

BEET AND EDAMAME SALAD 🌶🌶🌶

Beets have a reputation for being fussy to make, but the ready-to-eat steamed and peeled beets in this recipe are sweet and easy.

Bhut Jolokia

FRESH

PREP TIME: **5 MIN.** / TOTAL TIME: **10 MIN.** / SERVES: **8 (ABOUT 1½ CUPS)**

Vinaigrette

- 2 oranges, zested and juiced (about ⅔ cup juice)
- ½ cup seasoned rice vinegar
- 2 tablespoons agave syrup
- ¼ fresh bhut jolokia (ghost) chile pepper, stem and seeds removed, finely chopped

Salad

- 2 10-ounce packages shelled edamame
- 2 8-ounce packages peeled and steamed baby beets, diced

Salt

- ½ cup crumbled blue cheese (about 2 ounces)

1. To make vinaigrette, in a bowl, whisk together zest, juice, vinegar, agave, and chile.
2. To make salad, in a large bowl, combine edamame and beets; add vinaigrette and toss together. Season with salt to taste. Sprinkle with cheese. Serve.

Calories 200; **fat calories** 45; **total fat** 5g; **sat fat** 1.5g; **cholesterol** 5mg; **sodium** 460mg; **total carbohydrates** 25g; **fiber** 6g; **sugars** 15g; **protein** 10g; **vitamin A IUs** 10%; **vitamin C** 45%; **calcium** 10%; **iron** 10%

Cool It Down!

Try fresh red Fresno chiles instead of the bhut jolokia (ghost) chile pepper if you need a tamer salad.

Banana Wax

FRESH

QUINOA AND BLACK BEAN SALAD 🌶🌶

The ancient grain quinoa—botanically a relative of spinach—has become popular lately as a gluten-free alternative to other grains, with good reason: It's high in protein, minerals, and healthful omega oils.

PREP TIME: **30 MIN.** / TOTAL TIME: **40 MIN.** / SERVES: **8 (ABOUT 1½ CUPS)**

1⅓ cups water
½ cup quinoa
6 tablespoons extra-virgin olive oil
2 tablespoons white wine vinegar
1 tablespoon fresh lemon juice
1 tablespoon chopped fresh basil
1 teaspoon chopped fresh oregano leaves
2 garlic cloves, minced
1 fresh banana wax chile pepper, stem and seeds removed, finely diced (about ¼ cup)
1 15-ounce can black beans, drained and rinsed
1 English cucumber, diced
2 large Roma tomatoes, diced (about 1 cup)
2 green onions, thinly sliced (about ½ cup)
¼ cup sliced green olives
Salt
1 head butter lettuce, chopped

1. In a medium saucepan, bring 1⅓ cups water just to boiling. Add quinoa. Remove from heat and cover; let stand until tender, about 5 to 8 minutes.
2. In a large bowl, whisk together oil and next 6 ingredients (through chile).
3. Add beans, cucumber, tomato, green onions, and olives to oil mixture; toss together. Gently fold in quinoa; sprinkle with salt to taste. Spoon bean mixture evenly onto lettuce. Serve.

Calories 190; **fat calories** 110; **total fat** 12g; **sat fat** 1.5g; **cholesterol** 0mg; **sodium** 240mg; **total carbohydrates** 19g; **fiber** 5g; **sugars** 2g; **protein** 5g; **vitamin A IUs** 20%; **vitamin C** 30%; **calcium** 4%; **iron** 10%

BRUSSELS- AND KALE-SPROUT SALAD 🌶🌶🌶

Scorpion

FRESH

Kale sprouts are a hybrid of Russian Red kale and Brussels sprouts, and resemble tiny heads of kale. Their sweet peppery flavor and crisp texture pop against the citrusy lime vinaigrette and the blisteringly hot scorpion chile.

PREP TIME: **20 MIN.** / TOTAL TIME: **30 MIN.** / SERVES: **8 (ABOUT 2 CUPS)**

Vinaigrette
- ¼ cup extra-virgin olive oil
- ¼ cup white wine vinegar
- ½ teaspoon dried oregano, crushed
- 2 fresh limes, juiced (about ¼ cup)
- 1 garlic clove, minced
- ¼ fresh scorpion chile pepper, stem and seeds removed, finely diced

Salt

Salad
- 1 pound Brussels sprouts, trimmed
- ½ pound kale sprouts, trimmed and halved
- 2 large Asian pears, diced (about 1¾ cups)

1. To make vinaigrette, in a bowl, whisk together oil and next 5 ingredients (through chile). Season with salt to taste.

2. To make salad, using a cheese grater, shave Brussels sprouts (or shred in a food processor fitted with a grater plate). In a large bowl, combine Brussels sprouts, kale sprouts, and pears; add vinaigrette and toss together. Serve.

Calories 250; **fat calories** 180; **total fat** 21g; **sat fat** 3g; **cholesterol** 0mg; **sodium** 460mg; **total carbohydrates** 15g; **fiber** 2g; **sugars** 1g; **protein** 3g; **vitamin A IUs** 70%; **vitamin C** 120%; **calcium** 6%; **iron** 8%

Simple Swap
If you can't find kale sprouts, substitute chopped baby kale leaves.

CAPRESE SALAD
DE ARBOL 〞

Instead of presenting individual caprese de arbol stacks on salad or appetizer plates, you could serve one big salad on a party platter. With balsamic vinegar, you do get what you pay for, so it's best to use a high-quality brand to get that deep, rich flavor with less acid sting.

PREP TIME: **10 MIN.** / TOTAL TIME: **35 MIN.** / SERVES: **6 (ABOUT 1¾ CUP)**

- 6 tablespoons balsamic vinegar
- 2 tablespoons packed brown sugar
- 6 heirloom tomatoes, sliced (about 2 pounds)
- 1 pound fresh buffalo mozzarella cheese, thinly sliced
- ¼ cup packed large whole fresh basil leaves
- 2 dried de arbol chile peppers, stems and seeds removed, finely ground

Salt

1. In a small saucepan, heat vinegar and brown sugar over medium heat until sugar is dissolved, stirring constantly. Reduce heat; simmer 1 minute. Cool completely in refrigerator, about 20 minutes.
2. On individual plates, evenly layer tomato slices, cheese slices, and basil leaves. Sprinkle with chile and salt to taste. Drizzle with vinegar mixture. Serve.

Calories 303; **fat calories** 160; **total fat** 18g; **sat fat** 11g; **cholesterol** 60mg; **sodium** 54mg 54; **total carbohydrates** 20g; **fiber** 1g; **sugars** 16g; **protein** 13g; **vitamin A IUs** 6%; **vitamin C** 40%; **calcium** 4%; **iron** 4%

Make Ahead
Make the balsamic drizzle ahead of time and store tightly covered in the refrigerator for up to one week.

GRILLED SALSA SALAD 🌶️🌶️

Sweet and savory, this delicious salad is perfect for those summer months when the grill is always fired up.

PREP TIME: **15 MIN.** / TOTAL TIME: **35 MIN.** / SERVES: **8 (ABOUT 2 CUPS)**

Tepin

DRIED

6 large Roma tomatoes, halved lengthwise and seeded
3 limes, halved
3 garlic cloves, peeled
2 large avocados, halved lengthwise and pitted
1 large mango, halved lengthwise and seeded (do not peel)
1 sweet onion, thickly sliced
Extra-virgin olive oil
¼ cup chopped fresh cilantro
15 dried tepin chile peppers, ground
Salt
1 head butter lettuce

1. Preheat grill to medium heat. Brush tomato and next 5 ingredients (through onion) with oil. Place fruits and vegetables on grill rack; grill, rotating halfway through grilling to achieve even grill marks, about 3 to 5 minutes. Set limes aside.

2. Peel and finely dice remaining grilled fruits and vegetables. In a bowl, combine fruits and vegetables, cilantro, and chile; toss together. Squeeze in lime juice; sprinkle with salt to taste. Serve with butter lettuce leaves.

Calories 130; **fat calories** 45; **total fat** 4.5g; **sat fat** 0.5g; **cholesterol** 0mg; **sodium** 300mg; **total carbohydrates** 22g; **fiber** 4g; **sugars** 11g; **protein** 3g; **vitamin A IUs** 50%; **vitamin C** 70%; **calcium** 4%; **iron** 6%

Kitchen Savvy

To remove the "cheeks" of a mango, stand the mango firmly on end. Using a knife, slice ¼ inch from center of the mango. Repeat on the other side.

WEDGE SALAD WITH SPICY BLUE CHEESE DRESSING ,,

Pequin

DRIED

This classic salad gets a spicy remake with the tiny but powerful pequin chile pepper, which has over 50,000 Scoville heat units! Roquefort, known for its pungent flavor, is an excellent choice for the blue cheese.

PREP TIME: **25 MIN.** / TOTAL TIME: **45 MIN.** / SERVES: **8 (ABOUT 1½ CUPS)**

Dressing

- 1½ cups crumbled blue cheese (about 6 ounces)
- ½ cup plain full-fat Greek yogurt
- 3 tablespoons milk
- 2 tablespoons extra-virgin olive oil
- 10 dried pequin chile peppers, ground (about 1 tablespoon)
- 1 lemon, juiced (about 3 tablespoons)

Salt

Salad

- 1 head iceberg lettuce (about 2 pounds)
- ½ pound heirloom cherry tomatoes, halved (about 2 cups)
- 1 6.5-ounce jar marinated artichoke hearts, drained
- 1 3.8-ounce can sliced black olives, drained
- ½ red onion, very thinly sliced (about ½ cup)
- 4 slices thick bacon, cooked and crumbled

1. To make dressing, in a bowl, combine cheese and next 5 ingredients (through juice); stir in salt to taste.

2. To make salad, remove core and outer leaves of lettuce and discard. Cut lettuce lengthwise into eight wedges and place on individual plates. In a bowl, combine tomato, artichoke hearts, olives, and onion. Spoon tomato mixture evenly over wedges; top each wedge evenly with dressing and bacon. Serve.

Calories 225; **fat calories** 140; **total fat** 16g; **sat fat** 6g; **cholesterol** 20mg; **sodium** 540mg; **total carbohydrates** 15g; **fiber** 3g; **sugars** 5g; **protein** 9g; **vitamin A IUs** 25%; **vitamin C** 25%; **calcium** 15%; **iron** 4%

AMBROSIA SALAD WITH HEAT "

Add an additional thinly sliced jalapeño for even more heat. If desired, garnish with vanilla wafers or crumbled amaretto cookies.

PREP TIME: **35 MIN.** / TOTAL TIME: **50 MIN.** / SERVES: **12 (ABOUT 2 CUPS)**

1 pound tangerines, peeled and segmented (about 2 cups)

½ pound fresh strawberries, hulled and quartered (about 1½ cups)

3 3-ounce packages dried tart cherries (about 1½ cups)

2 bananas, sliced (about ⅔ cup)

1 pineapple, peeled, cored, and cubed (about 3 cups)

2 fresh jalapeño chile peppers, stems and seeds removed, finely diced, divided (about 3 tablespoons)

3 cups heavy cream

2 tablespoons granulated sugar

2 tablespoons powdered sugar, sifted

1 teaspoon pure vanilla extract

2 vanilla beans

2 cups mini marshmallows

1½ cups dried coconut chips, lightly toasted

1. Place the bowl of a mixer in the freezer to chill. In a bowl, combine tangerine, strawberries, cherries, banana, pineapple, and half of jalapeño chile.

2. Pour cream into chilled mixer bowl; add sugars and vanilla extract. Split vanilla beans lengthwise; scrape seeds into bowl and discard pods. Using whisk attachment, whip cream mixture until stiff peaks form, about 3 to 5 minutes. Gently fold in remaining jalapeño chile.

3. In parfait dishes, layer half of fruit mixture, half of marshmallows, half of coconut, and half of whipped cream. Repeat procedure with remaining fruit mixture, marshmallows, coconut, and whipped cream. Serve.

Calories 250; **fat calories** 250; **total fat** 27g; **sat fat** 14g; **cholesterol** 80mg; **sodium** 35mg; **total carbohydrates** 42g; **fiber** 7g; **sugars** 26g; **protein** 3g; **vitamin A IUs** 35%; **vitamin C** 80%; **calcium** 8%; **iron** 6%

TROPICAL SPINACH SALAD 🌶🌶🌶

Trinidad Scorpion

DRIED

Is there a pepper hotter than the infamous bhut jolokia (ghost) chile pepper that boasts a million Scoville heat units? You bet! Two peppers from the tropical island of Trinidad, the Butch T scorpion and the Moruga scorpion, tip the fiery scales at around 1.5 and 2 million Scoville heat units respectively.

PREP TIME: **25 MIN.** / TOTAL TIME: **1 HR. 5 MIN.** / SERVES: **6 (2 CUPS)**

Vinaigrette
- ½ dried Trinidad scorpion chile pepper, stem and seeds removed
- 1 cup fresh strawberries, hulled
- 1 tablespoon balsamic vinegar
- 1½ teaspoons brown sugar
- Salt
- Freshly ground black pepper

Salad
- 8 cups fresh baby spinach (about 1⅓ pounds)
- 1 cup fresh blueberries (about ½ pound)
- 1 cup fresh strawberries, hulled and quartered (about ½ pound)
- 1 cup walnuts, lightly toasted (about ¼ pound)
- ½ cup crumbled blue cheese crumbled (about 2 ounces)

1. To make vinaigrette, in a bowl, combine chile and water to cover until reconstituted, about 30 minutes. Drain.
2. Place chile, 1 cup strawberries, vinegar, and sugar in a blender; process until smooth. Stir in salt and black pepper to taste.
3. To make salad, in a large bowl, combine salad ingredients. Add vinaigrette; toss together. Serve.

Calories 230; **fat calories** 140; **total fat** 16g; **sat fat** 3g; **cholesterol** 10mg; **sodium** 210mg; **total carbohydrates** 16g; **fiber** 5g; **sugars** 6g; **protein** 9g; **vitamin A IUs** 35%; **vitamin C** 60%; **calcium** 10%; **iron** 15%

Cool It Down!
Substitute dried habanero peppers if you'd like— they'll seem as mild as bell peppers in comparison to the Trinidad scorpion pepper!

Savina Ruby Hot

DRIED

FRUIT COCKTAIL WITH ZIPPY SIMPLE SYRUP 𝄢𝄢𝄢

Garnish with fresh basil sprigs or mint for an elegant presentation.

PREP TIME: **20 MIN.** / TOTAL TIME: **55 MIN.** / SERVES: **4 (ABOUT 1 CUP)**

Make Ahead

Make the simple syrup up to three days in advance and store in the refrigerator.

¼ cup sugar
¼ cup cold water
¼ dried Savina Ruby Hot habanero chile pepper, stem and seeds removed, finely diced
½ cup pitted fresh cherries
½ cup green grapes, halved lengthwise
½ cup red grapes, halved lengthwise
1 12-ounce baby pineapple, peeled, cored, and finely diced
1 large Asian pear, cored and finely diced (about ¾ cup)
1 large nectarine, finely diced (about ¾ cup)

1. Combine sugar, ¼ cup water, and chile in a small saucepan over medium heat; bring just to boiling, stirring constantly. Cook until sugar is dissolved, stirring constantly, about 5 minutes. Cool completely, about 30 minutes.
2. In a bowl, combine cherries and next 5 ingredients (through nectarine); toss together. Drizzle with simple syrup. Serve.

Calories 130; **fat calories** 5; **total fat** 0g; **sat fat** 0g; **cholesterol** 0mg; **sodium** 0mg; **total carbohydrates** 32g; **fiber** 3g; **sugars** 18g; **protein** 1g; **vitamin A IUs** 10%; **vitamin C** 15%; **calcium** 2%; **iron** 2%

BELL PEPPER AND GRILLED TUNA STACKS

Bell Pepper

FRESH

The tuna will be most flavorful if very rare on the inside yet well seared on the outside. Use the freshest tuna possible; it should have only a faint aroma of salt and sea.

PREP TIME: **25 MIN.** / TOTAL TIME: **50 MIN.** / SERVES: **4 (1 STACK)**

1   fresh green bell pepper
1   fresh yellow bell pepper
1   fresh red bell pepper
½   pound sushi-grade tuna steak
2   tablespoons extra-virgin olive oil
½   teaspoon granulated garlic
Salt
Freshly ground white pepper
¼   cup mayonnaise
2   Roma tomatoes, finely chopped (about ⅔ cup)
1   rib celery, finely chopped (about ½ cup)
Balsamic vinegar

1. Preheat grill to high heat. Remove top and bottom of each bell pepper and carefully remove seed core. Slice each pepper crosswise into ½-inch-thick rings.

2. Brush tuna evenly with oil. Sprinkle evenly with garlic; sprinkle evenly with salt and white pepper to taste. Place tuna on grill rack; grill until surface is completely browned but steak is still firm to the touch, about 2 to 3 minutes per side. Remove from grill immediately. Cool completely, about 15 minutes.

3. Cut cooked tuna into medium dice. In a bowl, combine tuna, mayonnaise, tomato, and celery; toss together.

4. Make a stack containing 1 ring of each color of bell pepper; fill with one-fourth of tuna mixture. Drizzle evenly with balsamic vinegar. Repeat to make 4 stacks. Serve.

Calories 210; **fat calories** 100; **total fat** 12g; **sat fat** 2g; **cholesterol** 20mg; **sodium** 940mg; **total carbohydrates** 12g; **fiber** 3g; **sugars** 8g; **protein** 15g; **vitamin A IUs** 80%; **vitamin C** 200%; **calcium** 2%; **iron** 8%

STONE FRUIT AND SPRING MIX SALAD 🌶️🌶️

Serve this refreshing but spicy salad with grilled chicken or fish.

PREP TIME: **30 MIN.** / TOTAL TIME: **50 MIN.** / SERVES: **6 (¾ CUP)**

Pequin

DRIED

Bell Pepper

FRESH

Vinaigrette
- ¼ cup seasoned rice vinegar
- ¼ cup extra-virgin olive oil
- ¼ teaspoon salt
- 5 dried pequin chile peppers, ground

Salad
- 8 cups spring lettuce mix
- 4 baby cucumbers, sliced (about ½ pound)
- 2 large nectarines, sliced
- 2 large plums, sliced
- 1 large fresh yellow bell pepper, stem and seeds removed, sliced
- 1 large fresh red bell pepper, stem and seeds removed, sliced

1. To make vinaigrette, in a bowl, whisk together vinegar, olive oil, salt, and chile.

2. To make salad, in a large bowl, combine lettuce and remaining ingredients; toss together. Add half of vinaigrette, gently toss together, adding more to taste or reserving extra for another use. Serve.

Calories 190; **fat calories** 80; **total fat** 9g; **sat fat** 1.5g; **cholesterol** 0mg; **sodium** 150mg; **total carbohydrates** 26g; **fiber** 4g; **sugars** 10g; **protein** 3g; **vitamin A IUs** 100%; **vitamin C** 280%; **calcium** 6%; **iron** 15%

Simple Swap

This recipe has lots of room for variety. Try apricots with Damson plums or peaches with black plums, and try using arugula instead of the spring mix.

Thai

FRESH

CITRUSY CHICKEN AND PEACH SALAD 𝄃𝄃𝄃

Mini cucumbers—also called Israeli or Persian cucumbers—are especially crisp, and provide a cooling balance to the spicy hot Thai pepper.

PREP TIME: **15 MIN.** / TOTAL TIME: **20 MIN.** / SERVES: **6 (1½ CUPS)**

Simple Swap

If you can't find blood oranges in your local grocery store, substitute oranges or tangerines, often found more easily throughout the year.

Vinaigrette

- ¼ cup red wine vinegar
- 1 tablespoon honey
- ½ teaspoon salt
- ½ teaspoon freshly ground black pepper
- 2 oranges, juiced (about ⅔ cup)
- 2 limes, juiced (about ¼ cup)
- 1 blood orange, juiced (about ⅓ cup)
- 1 large lemon, juiced (about 3 tablespoons)
- 1 fresh Thai chile pepper, stem and seeds removed, finely diced

Salad

- 1 rotisserie chicken (about 1½ to 2 pounds), deboned and shredded
- ½ cup pecans, lightly toasted and chopped
- 3 peaches, peeled and sliced
- 3 Israeli or Persian cucumbers, trimmed and thinly sliced lengthwise (about 6 ounces)
- 2 hearts romaine lettuce, shredded (about 4 cups)

1. To make vinaigrette, in a bowl, whisk together vinegar and next 8 ingredients (through chile).

2. To make salad, in a bowl, combine chicken and next 4 ingredients (through lettuce); toss together. Add vinaigrette; toss together. Serve.

Calories 320; **fat calories** 130; **total fat** 15g; **sat fat** 2.5g; **cholesterol** 85mg; **sodium** 290mg; **total carbohydrates** 19g; **fiber** 3g; **sugars** 14g; **protein** 31g; **vitamin A IUs** 60%; **vitamin C** 60%; **calcium** 4%; **iron** 10%

ANTIPASTO SALAD

What a great showcase for colorful sweet bell peppers! If desired, use gold and purple bell peppers, too. And for extra pizzazz, a sprinkle of ground dried hot chile pepper is just the ticket.

Bell Pepper

FRESH

PREP TIME: **30 MIN.** / TOTAL TIME: **50 MIN.** / SERVES: **12 (ABOUT 1¼ CUPS)**

Vinaigrette
- ¼ cup seasoned rice vinegar
- 1 tablespoon Dijon mustard
- 2 teaspoons dried Italian seasoning, crushed
- 1 dried tomato, finely diced (about 1 tablespoon)
- 1 garlic clove, minced
- ½ cup canola oil

Salad
- 1 pound rotini pasta, cooked, rinsed with cold water, and cooled
- ½ pound cooked ham, cubed (about 2 cups)
- 5 ounces smoked mozzarella cheese, cubed
- ¼ pound hard salami, cubed (about ¾ cup)
- 3 ounces pepperoni, cut into strips (about ¾ cup)
- ½ cup pitted green olives
- ½ cup pitted black olives
- 1 fresh green bell pepper, stem and seeds removed, diced
- 1 fresh red bell pepper, stem and seeds removed, diced
- 1 fresh yellow bell pepper, stem and seeds removed, diced
- 1 small sweet onion, very thinly sliced

Salt
Freshly ground black pepper
Pepperoncini peppers (optional)

1. To make vinaigrette, in a bowl, combine vinegar and next 4 ingredients (through garlic). Add oil in a continuous stream, whisking continuously.

2. To make salad, in a bowl, combine pasta and next 10 ingredients (through onion); sprinkle with salt and black pepper to taste. Add vinaigrette and gently toss together. Top with pepperoncini peppers, if desired. Serve at room temperature.

Calories 390; **fat calories** 190; **total fat** 22g; **sat fat** 6g; **cholesterol** 35mg; **sodium** 1,025mg; **total carbohydrates** 36g; **fiber** 3g; **sugars** 4g; **protein** 15g; **vitamin A IUs** 10%; **vitamin C** 85%; **calcium** 10%; **iron** 13%

Mulato

DRIED

CHILE-HERB ROASTED POTATO SALAD 🌶

Smoky, sweet mulato peppers are similar to ancho chiles, but have a slight heat to them.

PREP TIME: **30 MIN.** / TOTAL TIME: **1 HR. 5 MIN.** / SERVES: **6 (1½ CUPS)**

Heat It Up!

To keep the smoky flavor but add some fire, try dried chipotle chile pepper instead of the dried mulato chile peppers.

2½ pounds Dutch yellow potatoes, halved
⅓ cup extra-virgin olive oil, divided
½ teaspoon salt
¼ teaspoon freshly ground black pepper
3 tablespoons sherry vinegar
1 tablespoon Dijon mustard
8 shallots, finely diced (about ⅓ cup)
2 dried mulato chile peppers, stems and seeds removed, finely ground (about 3 tablespoons)
¼ cup fresh thyme, chopped
¼ cup fresh rosemary, chopped

1. Preheat oven to 425°F. In a bowl, combine potatoes with 2 tablespoons oil; toss together. Sprinkle with salt and black pepper. Transfer to baking sheet; bake at 425°F until fork tender, about 25 to 35 minutes. Cool completely, about 30 minutes.
2. In a bowl, whisk together remaining oil, vinegar, mustard, shallots, and chile. Add potato, thyme, and rosemary; toss to coat. Serve.

Calories 180; **fat calories** 70; **total fat** 8g; **sat fat** 1g; **cholesterol** 0mg; **sodium** 270mg; **total carbohydrates** 26g; **fiber** 3g; **sugars** 2g; **protein** 3g; **vitamin A IUs** 4%; **vitamin C** 25%; **calcium** 2%; **iron** 8%

GRILLED STEAK AND POTATO SALAD

De Arbol — DRIED

Pasilla Negro — DRIED

If desired, zest the citrus before juicing and add it to the marinade.

PREP TIME: **15 MIN.** / TOTAL TIME: **2 HR. 55 MIN.** / SERVES: **10 (4 OUNCE STEAK)**

2½ pounds flank steak
1 cup extra-virgin olive oil, divided
½ cup soy sauce
¼ cup packed brown sugar
1 tablespoon dry mustard
2 tablespoons Worcestershire sauce
1 dash liquid smoke
4 limes, juiced (about ½ cup)
3 lemons, juiced (about ½ cup)
3 cloves garlic, minced
1 dried de arbol chile pepper, stem and seeds removed, finely ground (about 1 tablespoon)
1 small red onion, thinly sliced (about 1 cup)
2 pounds Dutch yellow potatoes, halved
3 dried pasilla negro chile peppers, stems and seeds removed (about 1 ounce)
Salt
3 ears fresh corn, husked and cleaned
¼ cup white wine vinegar
1 tablespoon Dijon mustard
1 chipotle chile pepper, canned in adobo sauce
Freshly ground black pepper
2 green onions, thinly sliced (about ½ cup)

1. Pierce steak several times with a fork. In a large zip-top plastic bag, combine steak, ½ cup oil, and next 10 ingredients (through red onion). Seal bag; turn bag several times to mix well and coat steak. Refrigerate 2 hours or overnight.
2. In a large saucepan, combine potato, pasilla negro chile, and cold water to cover. Bring to a boil. Reduce heat; add ½ teaspoon salt and simmer just until fork tender, about 8 to 10 minutes. Drain; finely chop chile.
3. Preheat grill to medium-high. Remove steak from zip-top plastic bag; discard marinade. Place steak on grill rack; grill until a meat thermometer inserted into thickest portion reads 155°F, turning once, about 12 to 15 minutes. Let rest for 10 minutes. Place corn on grill rack; grill until charred, turning often, about 7 minutes. Cut kernels from cobs. Cut steak against the grain into very thin slices.
4. Place vinegar, mustard, and chipotle chile in a blender. Process on lowest setting, slowly drizzling in remaining ½ cup oil, until vinaigrette forms. Stir in salt and black pepper to taste.
5. In a bowl, combine potatoes, pasilla negro chile, corn, and green onions; toss together. Add vinaigrette; toss together. Top with steak slices. Serve.

Calories 480; **fat calories** 220; **total fat** 25g; **sat fat** 6g; **cholesterol** 90mg; **sodium** 410mg; **total carbohydrates** 34g; **fiber** 4g; **sugars** 13g; **protein** 33g; **vitamin A IUs** 6%; **vitamin C** 60%; **calcium** 8%; **iron** 20%

**PULLED
BBQ CHICKEN
SANDWICHES**

sandwiches

PULLED BBQ CHICKEN SANDWICHES 〉〉〉

Add a delicious slaw of shredded cabbage, thinly sliced fresh bell peppers, cider vinegar, and honey, if desired.

PREP TIME: **45 MIN.** / TOTAL TIME: **1 HR. 40 MIN.** / SERVES: **6 (1 SANDWICH)**

- 2 pounds bone-in chicken thighs
- 2 teaspoons smoked paprika
- Salt
- Freshly ground black pepper
- ¼ cup extra-virgin olive oil, divided
- 1 sweet onion, chopped (1 cup)
- 2 garlic cloves, chopped
- ½ dried Savina Ruby Hot habanero chile pepper, stem and seeds removed
- ¾ cup sugar
- ¾ cup bourbon whiskey
- ½ cup seasoned rice vinegar
- ½ cup cider vinegar
- 1 Caribbean red papaya, peeled, seeded, and chopped (2½ pounds)
- 6 hamburger buns, toasted

1. Preheat oven to 350°F. Sprinkle skin side of chicken evenly with paprika, salt, and black pepper. Heat 2 tablespoons oil in a roasting pan over high heat. Cook chicken, skin side down, until golden brown, about 5 to 7 minutes. Flip chicken over.

2. Cover and bake at 350°F for 20 minutes; remove cover and bake until completely cooked through, about 10 to 15 minutes. Discard skin and bones; shred chicken.

3. Heat remaining 2 tablespoons oil in a large saucepan. Add onion; cook, stirring occasionally, 3 minutes. Add garlic and chile; cook, stirring, 30 seconds. Add sugar and next 4 ingredients (through papaya); bring just to boiling. Reduce heat; simmer until slightly thickened, about 15 minutes. Place onion mixture in a blender*; process until smooth.

4. In a medium saucepan, heat 2 cups sauce over medium heat (reserve remaining sauce for another use). Stir in chicken; cook until heated through, about 3 minutes. Spoon chicken mixture evenly onto bun bottoms; top with bun tops. Serve.

***Note:** Be cautious when blending hot foods; the contents expand rapidly, causing a risk of scalding. To be safe, before blending, remove center piece of blender lid (to allow steam to escape), secure lid on blender, and place a towel over opening in lid (to avoid splatters).*

Calories 470; **fat calories** 90; **total fat** 10g; **sat fat** 2g; **cholesterol** 85mg; **sodium** 400mg; **total carbohydrates** 54g; **fiber** 3g; **sugars** 28g; **protein** 22g; **vitamin A IUs** 10%; **vitamin C** 90%; **calcium** 10%; **iron** 15%

TUNA MELTS ✒

*The manzano chile pepper, whose name is derived from the Spanish word for "apple" (*manzana*), has distinctive black seeds.*

PREP TIME: **20 MIN.** / TOTAL TIME: **40 MIN.** / SERVES: **4 (1 SANDWICH)**

¼ cup sweet pickle relish
2 tablespoons mayonnaise
1 teaspoon red wine vinegar
2 5-ounce cans tuna packed in olive oil, drained
1 rib celery, finely diced (about ¼ cup)
Salt
Freshly ground black pepper
2 tablespoons unsalted butter, softened
8 slices sourdough bread
2 fresh manzano chile peppers, halved, stems and seeds removed, thinly sliced
4 slices sharp cheddar cheese

1. In a bowl, combine relish and next 4 ingredients (through celery); stir in salt and black pepper to taste.
2. Spread half of butter evenly on 4 bread slices. Place bread slices, buttered side down; top evenly with tuna mixture, chile, and cheese. Spread remaining butter on remaining 4 bread slices; place bread slices on top of cheese, buttered side up.
3. Heat a large skillet over medium heat. Cook 2 sandwiches at a time until golden brown and cheese is melted, about 5 minutes per side. Serve.

Calories 670; **fat calories** 200; **total fat** 23g; **sat fat** 8g; **cholesterol** 40mg; **sodium** 1,330mg; **total carbohydrates** 76g; **fiber** 5g; **sugars** 6g; **protein** 41g; **vitamin A IUs** 20%; **vitamin C** 110%; **calcium** 20%; **iron** 35%

Manzano

FRESH

Simple Swap

The manzano chile pepper is newly popular in the United States. If unavailable, substitute a serrano chile pepper—the spice level is about the same.

CRAB CAKE SANDWICHES ⟩

Shishito

Updated Maryland-style crab cakes get a hint of sizzle from shishito chile peppers. Padron chile peppers may be substituted.

FRESH

PREP TIME: **15 MIN.** / TOTAL TIME: **30 MIN.** / SERVES: **4 (1 SANDWICH)**

4 tablespoons canola oil, divided
12 fresh shishito chile peppers (about 2 ounces)
1 pound crabmeat, cleaned
1 cup panko (Japanese breadcrumbs)
¼ cup mayonnaise
1 tablespoon honey
2 garlic cloves, minced
1 large egg, slightly beaten
1 lime, juiced (about 2 tablespoons juice)
Salt
Freshly ground black pepper
1 cup Greek yogurt
3 tablespoons sweet pickle relish
4 Hawaiian sweet hamburger buns
Green leaf lettuce leaves (optional)
Sliced Roma tomato (optional)

1. Heat 1 tablespoon oil in a large skillet over medium-high heat; cook shishito chiles until blistered, turning several times, about 3 to 4 minutes. Cool until can be handled. Remove stems and seeds; finely chop chiles.
2. In a large bowl, gently combine chile and crabmeat. Gently stir in breadcrumbs and next 5 ingredients (through juice). Form crab mixture into 4 patties; sprinkle evenly with salt and black pepper.
3. Heat remaining 3 tablespoons oil in a large skillet over medium-high heat. Add patties; cook until golden brown, turning once, about 5 to 7 minutes. Transfer to paper towels to drain.
4. In a bowl, combine yogurt and relish. Spread yogurt mixture evenly on cut sides of bun halves. Top bun bottoms evenly with lettuce leaves, crab cakes, and tomato; top with bun tops. Serve.

Calories 620; **fat calories** 280; **total fat** 32g; **sat fat** 4g; **cholesterol** 135mg; **sodium** 870mg; **total carbohydrates** 47g; **fiber** 2g; **sugars** 11g; **protein** 38g; **vitamin A IUs** 6%; **vitamin C** 35%; **calcium** 25%; **iron** 10%

padron

FRESH

PEACH-PADRON GRILLED CHEESE SANDWICHES 🌶

Sweet peaches and bright green padron peppers add sunny flavors to this rustic sourdough grilled cheese sandwich.

PREP TIME: **10 MIN.** / TOTAL TIME: **20 MIN.** / SERVES: **4 (1 SANDWICH)**

Kitchen Savvy

For golden brown sandwiches, use a flat-bottomed cake pan or skillet to flatten sandwiches in the pan.

4 teaspoons olive oil, divided
8 fresh padron chile peppers, stems and seeds removed
Salt
Dijon mustard
8 large, thick slices sourdough bread
8 slices provolone cheese (about 12 ounces)
1 peach, thinly sliced

1. Heat 1 teaspoon oil in a small skillet over high heat; cook chiles until blistered and slightly wilted, turning several times, about 3 to 4 minutes. Sprinkle with salt to taste; transfer to paper towels.
2. Spread mustard evenly on bread slices. Place 1 slice cheese on mustard side of each of 4 bread slices; top evenly with peach, chiles, and remaining 4 cheese slices. Top with remaining bread slices, mustard side down. Brush sandwiches evenly with remaining 3 teaspoons oil.
3. Heat a large skillet over medium heat. Add sandwiches; cook until golden brown and cheese is melted, about 3 to 4 minutes per side. Cut each sandwich in half. Serve.

Calories 680; **fat calories** 180; **total fat** 20g; **sat fat** 9g; **cholesterol** 30mg; **sodium** 1,210mg; **total carbohydrates** 94g; **fiber** 5g; **sugars** 6g; **protein** 31g; **vitamin A IUs** 15%; **vitamin C** 45%; **calcium** 35%; **iron** 35%

PIMENTO-CHEESE BISCUIT SANDWICHES ⸝

Cherry Bell

FRESH

Enjoy these Southern-style party sandwiches with sparkling white wine or chilled lambic beer.

PREPARATION TIME: **20 MIN.** / TOTAL TIME: **35 MIN.** / SERVES: **10 (1 SANDWICH)**

1	can refrigerated buttermilk biscuit dough
8	ounces cream cheese, softened (about 1 cup)
½	cup shredded cheddar cheese (about 2 ounces)
¼	cup mayonnaise
½	teaspoon white pepper
¼	teaspoon salt
4	fresh cherry bell chile peppers, stems and seeds removed, finely diced (about ⅓ cup)
1	large shallot, finely diced (about 2 tablespoons)
¾	cup watercress or arugula

Fresh cherry bell chile peppers, thinly sliced (optional)

1. Bake biscuits according to package directions; cool to room temperature.

2. Place cheeses and next 5 ingredients (through shallot) in a food processor or blender; pulse to combine.

3. Cut biscuits in half. Top biscuit bottoms evenly with cheese mixture and watercress and sliced chiles, if desired. Top with biscuit tops. Serve.

Calories 200; **fat calories** 120; **total fat** 13g; **sat fat** 5g; **cholesterol** 25mg; **sodium** 420mg; **total carbohydrates** 17g; **fiber** 1g; **sugars** 2g; **protein** 5g; **vitamin A IUs** 8%; **vitamin C** 2%; **calcium** 6%; **iron** 6%

Make Ahead

Make the pimento cheese up to three days in advance and store in the refrigerator.

VEGETARIAN BÁNH MÌ SANDWICHES ⟩

Made with tofu, this is a vegetarian twist on the classic French-influenced Vietnamese sandwich.

Cherry Bell

FRESH

PREP TIME: **15 MIN.** / TOTAL TIME: **55 MIN.** / SERVES: **4 (1 PORTION SANDWICH)**

⅓ cup very thinly sliced daikon (about 2 ounces)

2 tablespoons lower-sodium soy sauce

1 tablespoon sesame oil

¼ teaspoon freshly ground black pepper

3 fresh cherry bell chile peppers, stems and seeds removed, thinly sliced (about ⅓ cup)

1 small carrot, thinly shredded (about ⅓ cup)

1 green onion, thinly sliced (about ¼ cup)

1 18-inch French baguette, cut in half lengthwise

¼ cup mayonnaise

¼ cup sweet chili sauce

2 6-ounce packages baked tofu or tofu cutlet, thinly sliced

¼ cup chopped fresh cilantro

¼ cup chopped fresh mint

1. In a bowl, combine daikon and next 6 ingredients (through green onion); let sit for at least 30 minutes.

2. Preheat oven to 325°F. Place baguette on a baking sheet; bake at 325°F until lightly toasted, about 10 to 12 minutes. Spread mayonnaise evenly on cut sides of baguette; spread chili sauce evenly over mayonnaise. Arrange tofu evenly on baguette bottom. Drain sliced vegetable mixture; arrange evenly over tofu. Sprinkle evenly with cilantro and mint; top with baguette top. Cut into 4 equal portions. Serve.

Calories 590; **fat calories** 310; **total fat** 35g; **sat fat** 5g; **cholesterol** 10mg; **sodium** 456mg; **total carbohydrates** 42g; **fiber** 4g; **sugars** 6g; **protein** 27g; **vitamin A IUs** 90%; **vitamin C** 15%; **calcium** 8%; **iron** 25%

Heat It Up!

This mild version of the *bánh mì* uses cherry bell peppers, but sliced fresh jalapeño chile peppers would add a welcome heat.

Bell Pepper

FRESH

Cubanelle

FRESH

OPEN-FACED GRILLED VEGGIE SANDWICHES ⟩

Try this sandwich with different vegetables, cheeses, or chiles.

PREP TIME: **20 MIN.** / TOTAL TIME: **41 MIN.** / SERVES: **10 (1 SANDWICH)**

Simple Swap

If you can't find chayote squash in your local grocery store, summer squash is closest in flavor.

7 tablespoons extra-virgin olive oil, divided
1 tablespoon unsalted butter
2 large sweet onions, halved and very thinly sliced (about 2 to 2½ cups)
2 fresh red bell peppers, stems and seeds removed, sliced into rounds
2 fresh green bell peppers, stems and seeds removed, sliced into rounds
1 pound cremini mushrooms, stems removed
2 chayote squash, halved lengthwise, seeded, and sliced
Olive oil cooking spray
Salt
Freshly ground black pepper
2 tablespoons cider vinegar
1 small shallot, finely diced (about 2 teaspoons)
1 garlic clove, minced
1 loaf ciabatta bread, halved lengthwise
4 fresh Cubanelle chile peppers, charred, peeled, stems and seeds removed, sliced into rounds (about ½ pound)
6 slices mozzarella cheese

1. Heat 1 tablespoon oil and butter in a large skillet over medium heat. Add onion; cook until browned, stirring once, about 10 to 12 minutes.

2. Preheat grill to medium-high heat. Lightly spray bell peppers, mushrooms, and chayote with cooking spray; sprinkle with salt and black pepper to taste. Place vegetables on grill rack; grill directly over heat until just tender, turning once, about 10 to 12 minutes.

3. In a bowl, whisk together remaining 6 tablespoons oil, vinegar, shallot, and garlic; whisk in salt and black pepper to taste.

4. Preheat broiler to high. Line a baking sheet with foil. Brush vinegar mixture evenly on cut sides of bread halves; arrange on prepared baking sheet, cut sides up. Arrange mushrooms, chayote, bell peppers, onion, and chile evenly on both bread halves; top with cheese. Broil until cheese is melted and sandwiches are heated through, about 1 to 2 minutes. Cut each bread half into 5 pieces. Serve.

Calories 370; **fat calories** 180; **total fat** 20g; **sat fat** 8g; **cholesterol** 30mg; **sodium** 430mg; **total carbohydrates** 36g; **fiber** 5g; **sugars** 9g; **protein** 14g; **vitamin A IUs** 50%; **vitamin C** 350%; **calcium** 25%; **iron** 15%

PORTOBELLO GRILLED CHEESE SANDWICHES ″

Cascabel

DRIED

Balance this flavor-packed sandwich with a light, crisp fruit salad.

PREP TIME: **35 MIN.** / TOTAL TIME: **1 HR. 21 MIN.** / SERVES: **4 (1 SANDWICH)**

Pesto
- 3 dried Cascabel chile peppers, stems and seeds removed
- 2 cups packed fresh basil leaves
- ¼ cup slivered almonds, lightly toasted
- 2 garlic cloves, peeled
- 1 lemon, juiced (about 3 tablespoons juice)
- ⅔ cup extra-virgin olive oil
- ½ cup grated Parmesan cheese (about 2 ounces)
- ¼ teaspoon salt
- ¼ teaspoon freshly ground black pepper

Sandwiches
- 4 large portobello mushrooms, stems removed (about 1¼ pounds)
- Olive oil
- 4 tablespoons unsalted butter, softened (¼ cup)
- 8 slices sourdough bread
- 4 1-ounce slices smoked mozzarella cheese
- ¼ cup sun-dried tomatoes
- 1 cup packed fresh spinach leaves (3 to 4 ounces)

1. To make pesto, soak chiles in cold water until rehydrated, 30 minutes; drain. Place chiles, basil, almonds, garlic, and juice in a blender; process on low until almost smooth, gradually drizzling in ⅔ cup oil. Spoon into a bowl; stir in cheese, salt, and black pepper.

2. To make sandwiches, preheat grill to medium-high heat. Brush mushrooms with oil. Place on grill rack; grill until slightly softened, about 5 minutes per side.

3. Spread half of butter evenly on 4 bread slices; spread 1 tablespoon pesto evenly on opposite sides. Top pesto side evenly with cheese slices, mushrooms, tomato, and spinach. Spread remaining butter on remaining 4 bread slices; place bread slices on top of spinach, buttered side up.

4. Heat a large skillet over medium heat. Add sandwiches; cook until golden brown on both sides and cheese is melted, about 3 to 5 minutes per side. Serve.

Calories 780; **fat calories** 430; **total fat** 48g; **sat fat** 19g; **cholesterol** 80mg; **sodium** 100mg; **total carbohydrates** 63g; **fiber** 5g; **sugars** 8g; **protein** 30g; **vitamin A IUs** 40%; **vitamin C** 25%; **calcium** 50%; **iron** 25%

Kitchen Savvy
Keep large batches of toasted nuts in the freezer for faster preparation.

GRILLED VEGETABLE-CHILE POCKET PIZZAS ▶▶

Stuff the best flavors of a veggie pizza into a pita pocket!

Tepin

‖‖‖‖‖‖‖‖‖‖‖‖‖‖‖‖

DRIED

‖‖‖‖‖‖‖‖‖‖‖‖‖‖‖‖

PREP TIME: **1 HR.** / TOTAL TIME: **1 HR. 50 MIN.** / SERVES: **8 (½ PITA ROUND)**

2 zucchini, trimmed and sliced lengthwise (about 1¼ pounds)
2 yellow squash, trimmed and sliced lengthwise (about 1¼ pounds)
2 portobello mushrooms, stems and gills removed
1 sweet onion, sliced
3 tablespoons extra-virgin olive oil, divided
Salt
Freshly ground black pepper
½ sweet onion, finely diced
4 large Roma tomatoes, chopped (about 1½ cups)
2 garlic cloves, minced
15 dried tepin chile peppers, crushed (about 2 tablespoons)
2 tablespoons tomato paste
2 teaspoons sugar
2 teaspoons dried oregano, crushed
½ teaspoon chili powder
¼ cup fresh basil leaves, finely chopped
4 6-inch pita bread rounds, split
12 ounces sliced mozzarella cheese

1. Preheat grill to medium-high heat. Brush zucchini, squash, mushrooms, and sliced onion with 2 tablespoons oil; sprinkle evenly with salt and pepper. Place vegetables on grill rack; grill until marked and just cooked through, flipping once, about 10 to 12 minutes. Cool until can be handled; cut vegetables into strips.

2. Heat remaining 1 tablespoon oil in a large saucepan over medium-high heat. Add finely diced onion; cook until translucent, stirring occasionally, about 5 minutes. Stir in tomato, garlic, and tepin chile. Reduce heat; simmer 5 minutes. Add tomato paste, sugar, oregano, chili powder, and salt. Simmer 15 minutes, stirring often. Stir in basil.

3. Spread about 1 tablespoon of tomato mixture on 4 of the split pita rounds. Top evenly with vegetables and cheese; top with remaining split rounds. Place sandwiches on grill rack; grill just until cheese is melted, about 1 to 2 minutes per side. Cut pita rounds in half. Serve.

Calories 410; **fat calories** 150; **total fat** 17g; **sat fat** 7g; **cholesterol** 25mg; **sodium** 590mg; **total carbohydrates** 46g; **fiber** 4g; **sugars** 9g; **protein** 18g; **vitamin A IUs** 30%; **vitamin C** 60%; **calcium** 40%; **iron** 16%

Kitchen Savvy
Use jarred marinara sauce if short on time.

EGG SALAD SANDWICHES WITH PEPPER RELISH 🌶

White and black peppercorns come from the same plant; white peppercorns have had the outer skin removed.

PREP TIME: **25 MIN.** / TOTAL TIME: **30 MIN.** / SERVES: **4 (1 SANDWICH)**

Relish
- 2 fresh shishito chile peppers, stems and seeds removed, finely diced
- 2 tablespoons finely diced dill pickles
- 1 tablespoon finely diced green onion (white part only)
- 1 tablespoon finely diced celery

Salt

White pepper

Egg Salad
- 6 large eggs, hardboiled and finely chopped
- 3 tablespoons mayonnaise
- ¼ teaspoon wasabi powder

Salt

- 4 Hawaiian bread mini-sub rolls, cut in half

1. To make relish, in a bowl, combine chile, pickle, green onion, and celery; stir in salt and white pepper to taste.

2. To make egg salad, in a bowl, combine eggs, mayonnaise, and wasabi powder; stir in salt to taste.

3. Spoon egg salad evenly onto roll bottoms; top evenly with relish. Top with roll tops. Serve.

Calories 370; **fat calories** 170; **total fat** 19g; **sat fat** 4g; **cholesterol** 285mg; **sodium** 670mg; **total carbohydrates** 36g; **fiber** 5g; **sugars** 7g; **protein** 16g; **vitamin A IUs** 20%; **vitamin C** 20%; **calcium** 15%; **iron** 15%

Cool It Down!

This sandwich has a little touch of heat; to tone down the intensity, omit the wasabi powder.

TURKEY-AND-SAUSAGE MEATBALL SANDWICHES 🌶

Padron

FRESH

Meatball sandwiches are the perfect food to eat while watching your favorite sporting events.

PREP TIME: **30 MIN.** / TOTAL TIME: **55 MIN.** / SERVES: **6 (1 SANDWICH)**

- ½ **pound lean ground turkey**
- ½ **pound ground sweet Italian sausage**
- ½ **cup Italian breadcrumbs**
- ¼ **cup finely grated Parmesan cheese (about 1 ounce)**
- 2 **teaspoons tomato paste**
- 2 **garlic cloves, minced**
- 1 **large egg**

Salt

Freshly ground white pepper

- 2 **tablespoons extra-virgin olive oil**
- 2 **cups sliced button mushrooms**
- 8 **fresh padron chile peppers, halved, stems and seeds removed**
- 1 **small red onion, halved and thinly sliced (about 1 cup)**
- 1 **24-ounce jar marinara sauce**
- 6 **French rolls, halved lengthwise**
- 12 **ounces sliced mozzarella cheese**

1. Preheat oven to 400°F. Lightly spray a baking sheet with cooking spray. In a bowl, combine turkey and next 6 ingredients (through egg); stir in salt and white pepper. Form turkey mixture into 1-inch meatballs.

2. Arrange meatballs in a single layer on prepared baking sheet. Bake at 400°F until completely cooked through, about 15 to 20 minutes. Keep oven at 400°F.

3. Heat oil in a saucepan over medium-high heat. Add mushroom, chile, and onion; cook until onion is softened and mushrooms have released their liquid, stirring occasionally, about 10 minutes. Stir in marinara sauce. Reduce heat; simmer until heated through.

4. Remove some of the insides of French rolls to form a trench for the meatballs. Arrange roll halves on a baking sheet, cut sides up; top evenly with meatballs, sauce mixture, and mozzarella cheese. Bake at 400°F until cheese melts, about 5 minutes. Serve.

Calories 740; **fat calories** 330; **total fat** 37g; **sat fat** 14g; **cholesterol** 125mg; **sodium** 1,920mg; **total carbohydrates** 61g; **fiber** 7g; **sugars** 11g; **protein** 40g; **vitamin A IUs** 20%; **vitamin** C 90%; **calcium** 60%; **iron** 30%

Make Ahead

Bake the meatballs the day before and store in a tightly covered container in the refrigerator. When ready to serve, reheat in the oven for 10 minutes.

Hungarian Wax

FRESH

TURKEY BURGERS WITH CRANBERRY-LIME MAYO ⟩

These turkey burgers have it all: a little bit of sweet, a little bit of spicy, and lots of savory.

PREP TIME: **15 MIN.** / TOTAL TIME: **30 MIN.** / SERVES: **4 (1 BURGER)**

Simple Swap

Substitute ground chicken for the turkey, if desired.

1   pound lean ground turkey
¼   cup barbecue sauce
1   large fresh Hungarian wax chile pepper, stem and seeds removed, diced
2   garlic cloves, minced
Salt
Freshly ground black pepper
Vegetable oil
1   cup mayonnaise
¼   cup dried cranberries, finely chopped
1   small lime, juiced (about 1½ tablespoons juice)
4   hamburger buns, toasted

1. In a large bowl, combine turkey, barbecue sauce, chile, and garlic; stir in salt and black pepper. Form turkey mixture into 4 patties, each about ¾ inch thick.

2. Preheat grill to medium-high heat. Oil grill rack. Place turkey patties on grill rack; grill until patties are cooked completely through and a meat thermometer inserted into thickest portion reads 165°F, turning once about halfway through, about 12 to 15 minutes.

3. In a bowl, combine mayonnaise, cranberries, and juice. Place 1 burger patty on each toasted bun bottom; top evenly with mayonnaise mixture. Top with bun tops. Serve.

Calories 495; **fat calories** 231; **total fat** 25g; **sat fat** 3.5g; **cholesterol** 55mg; **sodium** 492mg; **total carbohydrates** 35g; **fiber** 3g; **sugars** 10g; **protein** 33g; **vitamin A IUs** 45%; **vitamin C** 76%; **calcium** 8%; **iron** 16%

HATCH CHILE-TRI-TIP SANDWICHES))

Hatch

FRESH

Top off this Chicago-style Italian beef sandwich with your favorite condiments and add lettuce, tomato, and onion, if desired.

PREP TIME: **30 MIN.** / TOTAL TIME: **8 HR.** / SERVES: **6 (1 SANDWICH)**

¾ cup packed brown sugar
½ cup soy sauce
½ cup extra-virgin olive oil
2 tablespoons freshly ground black pepper
1 tablespoon dry mustard
2 tablespoons Worcestershire sauce
1 dash liquid smoke
4 limes, juiced (about ½ cup juice)
2½ lemons, juiced (about ½ cup juice)
3 garlic cloves, minced
1 red onion, sliced
2½ pounds beef tri-tip
6 fresh bakery rolls, cut in half
6 fresh Hatch chile peppers, roasted, peeled, stems and seeds removed

1. In a large bowl, whisk together brown sugar and next 10 ingredients (through red onion). In a large zip-top plastic bag, combine beef and brown sugar mixture. Seal bag; turn bag several times to mix well and coat beef. Refrigerate 8 hours or overnight.

2. Preheat grill to medium-high heat. Remove meat from zip-top plastic bag; discard marinade. Place meat on grill rack; grill until both sides are marked. Turn off all but one burner; move meat to cool side of grill rack and partially cover. Grill until desired doneness (125°F for rare, 135°F for medium, or 145°F for well done). Let meat rest 15 minutes. Slice thinly against the grain.

3. Top each bottom roll evenly with beef slices and 1 chile; top with roll tops. Serve.

Calories 820; **fat calories** 460; **total fat** 51g; **sat fat** 17g; **cholesterol** 285mg; **sodium** 1,230mg; **total carbohydrates** 42g; **fiber** 2g; **sugars** 19g; **protein** 49g; **vitamin A IUs** 25%; **vitamin C** 260%; **calcium** 10%; **iron** 30%

SAUSAGE AND PEPPER SANDWICHES

Garnish each sandwich with additional fresh basil leaves for more floral flavor.

PREP TIME: **25 MIN.** / TOTAL TIME: **45 MIN.** / SERVES: **4 (1 SANDWICH)**

- 4 sweet and/or spicy Italian sausages (1 pound)
- 2 tablespoons extra-virgin olive oil
- 2 sweet onions, halved and very thinly sliced (about 1½ cups)
- 1 pound fresh veggie sweet mini peppers, stems and seeds removed, sliced into thin rounds (about 3 cups)
- ¼ cup cooking sherry
- 2 tablespoons water
- ¼ teaspoon salt
- ¼ teaspoon freshly ground black pepper
- 2 garlic cloves, minced
- ¼ cup fresh basil chiffonade (sliced into thin ribbons)
- Spicy brown mustard (optional)
- 4 multigrain hoagie rolls, halved lengthwise

1. Heat a large skillet over medium-high heat. Add sausages; sear on all sides. Transfer sausages to a plate.

2. Add oil to skillet. Add onion; cook until browned, stirring once, about 7 to 10 minutes. Add sausages, mini peppers, and next 5 ingredients (through garlic); cook until sausages are cooked through completely, stirring occasionally, about 10 minutes. Remove from heat; stir in basil.

3. Spread mustard evenly on cut sides of rolls, if desired. Top bottom roll half evenly with sausage mixture; top with roll tops. Serve.

Calories 640; **fat calories** 300; **total fat** 33g; **sat fat** 10g; **cholesterol** 55mg; **sodium** 1,230mg; **total carbohydrates** 60g; **fiber** 7g; **sugars** 15g; **protein** 25g; **vitamin A IUs** 10%; **vitamin C** 170%; **calcium** 15%; **iron** 20%

Heat It Up!
Crank up the spice with sliced fresh red Fresno chile pepper.

STUFFED ROASTED PORK TENDERLOIN

main dishes

STUFFED ROASTED PORK TENDERLOIN

To get the most intense flavor from cumin, toast whole seeds, cool, and grind.

PREP TIME: **40 MIN.** / TOTAL TIME: **1 HR. 45 MIN.** / SERVES: **8 (4 TO 6 OUNCES)**

¼   pound ground sweet Italian sausage

2   tablespoons extra-virgin olive oil

1   tablespoon unsalted butter

½   yellow onion, diced

1   24-ounce pork tenderloin

1   tablespoon chili powder

1   tablespoon ground cumin

½   teaspoon salt

¼   teaspoon freshly ground black pepper

8   fresh veggie sweet mini peppers, charred, stems and seeds removed, sliced into rings

1   small Granny Smith apple, finely diced (about ½ cup)

½   cup chicken broth

1. Heat a large skillet over medium-high heat. Add sausage; cook until sausage is browned, stirring occasionally, about 7 to 10 minutes. Transfer to paper towels to drain.

2. Add oil and butter to hot skillet. Add onion; cook until golden, stirring once, about 7 minutes.

3. Preheat oven to 350°F. Slice tenderloin lengthwise all but ½ inch through and press it flat (butterfly). Sprinkle evenly with chili powder, cumin, salt, and black pepper. Top with sausage, onion, mini peppers, and apple. Roll tenderloin up, jelly-roll style, and secure with butcher's twine or seal with toothpicks. Reheat skillet over medium-high heat. Add tenderloin; cook until seared, turning once, about 5 minutes per side.

4. Transfer stuffed tenderloin to rack of a roasting pan. Add broth to pan and cover with foil. Roast at 350°F until a meat thermometer inserted into thickest portion reads 160°F, removing foil for the last 10 minutes, about 40 minutes. Transfer pork to a carving board; let rest 10 minutes. Cut tenderloin into 8 slices. Serve.

Calories 140; **fat calories** 100; **total fat** 11g; **sat fat** 3g; **cholesterol** 15mg; **sodium** 125mg; **total carbohydrates** 7g; **fiber** 1g; **sugars** 3g; **protein** 3g; **vitamin A IUs** 6%; **vitamin C** 40%; **calcium** 2%; **iron** 2%

GREEK-STYLE PASTA ALFREDO WITH SHRIMP 〃

Guajillo

_____

DRIED

_____

Serve with a lemon and olive oil–dressed Greek salad.

PREP TIME: **20 MIN.** / TOTAL TIME: **1 HR.** / SERVES: **8**

1   14-ounce package dried fettuccini
2½ teaspoons dried oregano, crushed
2   teaspoons dried thyme, crushed
1   teaspoon dried granulated garlic
1   teaspoon dried marjoram, crushed
1   teaspoon dried basil, crushed
2   pounds raw shrimp, peeled and deveined
2   tablespoons extra-virgin olive oil
2   tablespoons unsalted butter
4   dried guajillo chile peppers, stems and seeds removed
2   garlic cloves, minced
1   sweet onion, finely diced (about ⅔ cup)
½   teaspoon salt
¼   teaspoon freshly ground black pepper
1   cup dry white wine
½   cup whole milk
1   8-ounce container plain Greek yogurt
1½ cups grated Parmesan cheese (about 6 ounces)
1   14.5-ounce can diced tomatoes, drained
1   3.8-ounce can sliced black olives, drained

1. Cook pasta according to package directions; drain.

2. In a bowl, combine oregano and next 4 ingredients (through basil). Add shrimp; toss together.

3. Heat oil and butter in a large straight-sided sauté pan over medium-high heat. Add shrimp; cook until pink and just cooked through, about 2 to 3 minutes per side. Remove shrimp. Add chiles and next 4 ingredients (through black pepper) to sauté pan; cook 30 seconds.

4. Stir in wine, milk, and yogurt. Gradually stir in cheese; cook until cheese is melted, stirring constantly, about 5 minutes. Stir in tomatoes and olives. Remove chiles; finely dice and return to sauté pan. Reduce heat; simmer 10 minutes. Add shrimp during last 2 minutes to heat through.

5. Add pasta to sauté pan; gently toss together. Serve.

Calories 600; **fat calories** 160; **total fat** 18g; **sat fat** 7g; **cholesterol** 175mg; **sodium** 1,260mg; **total carbohydrates** 70; **fiber** 2g; **sugars** 6g; **protein** 36g; **vitamin A IUs** 60%; **vitamin C** 20%; **calcium** 40%; **iron** 10%

LOBSTER-CHILE MAC 'N' CHEESE ""

Cayenne

FRESH

This ultimate comfort dish can easily be made in individual baking dishes, but be sure to cut the baking time in half.

PREP TIME: **40 MIN.** / TOTAL TIME: **1 HR. 30 MIN.** / SERVES: **10 (ABOUT 2 CUPS)**

1	pound elbow macaroni
4	cups whole milk
4	tablespoons unsalted butter (¼ cup)
½	cup all-purpose flour
1	fresh cayenne chile pepper, stem and seeds removed, thinly sliced
1½	cups shredded Jack cheese (about 6 ounces)
1½	cups shredded sharp cheddar cheese (about 6 ounces)
1½	teaspoons smoked paprika
1½	pounds cooked lobster meat, chopped (about 3 cups)
Salt	

1. Preheat oven to 375°F. Cook pasta according to package directions; drain. In a small saucepan over medium-high heat, bring milk just to scalding (small bubbles just appear around edge of saucepan).

2. Melt butter in a large saucepan over medium-high heat. Slowly whisk in flour, stirring constantly until a thick paste (roux) forms. Slowly whisk in scalded milk and chile. Reduce heat to medium-low; simmer until slightly thickened, about 5 minutes. Remove from heat; stir in cheeses, paprika, pasta, and lobster. Stir in salt to taste.

3. Spoon pasta mixture into a 5-quart baking dish. Bake at 375°F until browned on top and sauce is bubbly, about 30 to 35 minutes. Serve.

Calories 460; **fat calories** 150; **total fat** 17g; **sat fat** 10g; **cholesterol** 95mg; **sodium** 520mg; **total carbohydrates** 45g; **fiber** 2g; **sugars** 6g; **protein** 31g; **vitamin A IUs** 20%; **vitamin C** 0%; **calcium** 40%; **iron** 10%

Simple Swap

Swap the lobster for an equivalent amount of chopped cooked shrimp, crawfish, or even scallops.

LEMON-LIME SHRIMP AND SHISHITO PEPPERS 🌶

Shishito chile peppers come with a surprise: Some are hot and some are mild, even when from the same plant.

PREP TIME: **10 MIN.** / TOTAL TIME: **33 MIN.** / SERVES: **6**

3	limes, juiced (about ⅓ cup juice)
2	lemons, juiced (about ⅓ cup juice)
2	teaspoons granulated garlic
1	pound raw shrimp, peeled and deveined
2	tablespoons peanut oil or extra-virgin olive oil
30	fresh shishito chile peppers, (about 6 ounces)
¼	cup soy sauce

Hot cooked rice or rice noodles (optional)

1. In a large bowl, combine juices and garlic. Add shrimp; toss together. Let sit 10 minutes.

2. Heat oil in a wok or large skillet over medium-high heat; add chiles. Cook until charred on all sides, turning as needed, about 7 to 10 minutes. Add shrimp and marinade; cook until opaque and slightly pink and just cooked through, about 5 minutes. Stir in soy sauce; cook 1 minute. Spoon over hot cooked rice or rice noodles, if desired. Serve.

Calories 120; **fat calories** 50; **total fat** 5g; **sat fat** 1g; **cholesterol** 95mg; **sodium** 960g; **total carbohydrates** 8g; **fiber** 1g; **sugars** 2g; **protein** 12g; **vitamin A IUs** 10%; **vitamin C** 90%; **calcium** 4%; **iron** 2%

Ancho

DRIED

CHILES TOLUCOS

This recipe is similar to chiles rellenos but uses dried chiles instead.

PREP TIME: **55 MIN.** / TOTAL TIME: **1 HR. 30 MIN.** / SERVES: **6 (1 CHILE)**

2	quarts water
6	dried ancho chile peppers
1	cup orange juice
½	cup cider vinegar
5	garlic cloves, minced
2	piloncillo (Mexican brown sugar cone) or 1½ cups dark brown sugar
1	teaspoon dried oregano, crushed
1	teaspoon dried thyme, crushed
2	tablespoons canola oil
¼	pound Soyrizo
1	cup purchased refried beans
¼	teaspoon salt
3	cups grated Manchego cheese (about 12 ounces), divided
1	cup crema or sour cream

1. In a large saucepan, bring 2 quarts water just to boiling; remove from heat. Add chiles; soak until softened, about 20 minutes. Drain; cool until can be handled. Make a lengthwise cut along the side of each chile and carefully remove seeds and veins.
2. In a medium saucepan, combine juice and vinegar. Bring just to a simmer, about 5 minutes. Stir in garlic, piloncillo, oregano, and thyme; cook until piloncillo dissolves. Remove from heat; add chiles. Let sit 20 minutes. Transfer chiles to a paper towel–lined plate. Strain mixture; discard solids.

3. In a large skillet, heat oil over medium heat. Add Soyrizo; cook until heated through, about 5 minutes. Stir in beans and salt.
4. Preheat oven to 350°F. Carefully stuff chiles evenly with 2 cups cheese and Soyrizo mixture. Arrange seam side down in a baking dish. Spoon crema on top; sprinkle with remaining 1 cup cheese. Bake at 350°F until cheese is melted, about 15 minutes. Serve with warm vinegar mixture.

Calories 800; **fat calories** 330; **total fat** 37g; **sat fat** 20g; **cholesterol** 65mg; **sodium** 830mg; **total carbohydrates** 94g; **fiber** 3g; **sugars** 14g; **protein** 21g; **vitamin A IUs** 160%; **vitamin C** 40%; **calcium** 70%; **iron** 10%

BROCCOLI-FLOWER CHILE MAC 》

A pair of piquant cayenne chile peppers adds spice to this vegetable-studded mac 'n' cheese.

Cayenne

FRESH

PREP TIME: **30 MIN.** / TOTAL TIME: **1 HR. 5 MIN.** / SERVES: **10 (ABOUT 2 CUPS)**

¾ cup broccoli florets, cut into bite-size pieces
¾ cup cauliflower florets, cut into bite-size pieces
1 16-ounce package elbow macaroni
4 tablespoons unsalted butter (¼ cup)
¼ cup all-purpose flour
4 cups whole milk
½ teaspoon salt
2 fresh cayenne chile peppers, stems and seeds removed, finely chopped
1 cup whole-milk ricotta cheese
1 cup shredded sharp cheddar cheese (about 4 ounces)
⅓ cup grated Parmesan cheese (about 1.5 ounces)
1½ cups Italian breadcrumbs

1. Preheat oven to 375°F. Bring a large saucepan of salted water just to boiling. Add vegetables; cook 3 minutes. Transfer vegetables to a bowl of ice water; drain. Cook pasta according to package directions; drain.

2. Melt butter in a large saucepan over medium-high heat; whisk in flour until a thick paste (roux) forms. Whisk in milk, salt, and chile. Bring mixture just to boiling. Reduce heat; simmer until slightly thickened, about 5 minutes. Remove from heat; stir in cheeses until melted. Fold in pasta.

3. Fold broccoli and cauliflower into pasta and cheese mixture; spoon into a 5-quart baking dish. Top with breadcrumbs; bake at 375°F until warmed through, about 15 to 20 minutes. Serve.

Calories 456; **fat calories** 160; **total fat** 18g; **sat fat** 10g; **cholesterol** 52mg; **sodium** 656mg; **total carbohydrates** 56g; **fiber** 2g; **sugars** 7g; **protein** 19g; **vitamin A IUs** 16%; **vitamin C** 16%; **calcium** 36%; **iron** 16%

Jalapeño

FRESH

ENCHILADAS SUIZAS 🌶🌶

Sweet potatoes are a surprising, earthy addition to these cheesy ("suizas") enchiladas.

PREP TIME: **30 MIN.** / TOTAL TIME: **1 HR. 35 MIN.** / SERVES: **5 (2 ENCHILADAS)**

Simple Swap
If you can't find white or yellow sweet potatoes, yams will do in a pinch.

1 pound yellow or white sweet potatoes, peeled and sliced into ¼-inch-thick slabs
4 fresh jalapeño chile peppers
¼ cup extra-virgin olive oil, divided
Salt
Freshly ground black pepper
1 white onion, finely diced
3 garlic cloves, minced
4 cups fresh spinach, chopped
1 tablespoon all-purpose flour
1 cup whole milk
1 cup crema or sour cream
1⅓ cups shredded Jack cheese, divided
10 6-inch corn tortillas

1. Preheat oven to 350°F. Arrange potato and chiles in a single layer on a baking sheet. Drizzle evenly with 1 tablespoon oil; sprinkle with salt and black pepper. Bake at 350°F until potatoes are tender, turning once halfway through, about 20 to 24 minutes. Cool until can be handled, about 20 minutes. Remove stems and seeds from chiles; finely chop.
2. Increase oven temperature to 375°F. Heat 2 tablespoons oil in a large skillet over medium heat. Add onion; cook until softened, stirring occasionally, about 10 minutes. Add garlic; cook 2 minutes. Add spinach; add salt

and black pepper to taste. Toss together. Cover; cook until spinach is wilted, about 2 to 3 minutes.
3. Heat remaining 1 tablespoon oil in a large straight-sided sauce-pan. Add flour; cook, stirring constantly, 3 minutes. Stir in milk, crema, and chopped chile. Stir in ⅔ cup cheese; cook until cheese is melted completely and mixture is smooth, stirring constantly.
4. Coat a 13 x 9–inch baking dish with cooking spray. Using metal tongs, slightly char tortillas over the open flame of a gas burner, about 10 seconds per side, or microwave until soft (this will make them easier to roll). Fill tortillas evenly with ⅓ cup cheese, potato, and spinach mixture. Roll filled tortillas as you prepare, arranging seam side down and side by side in prepared baking dish.
5. Pour sauce over enchiladas. Cover with foil; bake at 375°F for 20 minutes. Remove foil; sprinkle with remaining ⅓ cup cheese. Bake untilcheese is melted, 5 to 7 minutes. Serve.

Calories 570; **fat calories** 270; **total fat** 30g; **sat fat** 15g; **cholesterol** 70mg; **sodium** 820mg; **total carbohydrates** 59g; **fiber** 7g; **sugars** 11g; **protein** 16g; **vitamin A IUs** 340%; **vitamin C** 110%; **calcium** 25%; **iron** 8%

CHILE-BASIL
PESTO

CHILE-BASIL PESTO ,,

The arrabbiata (spicy) version of this Genoese classic is a perfect partner for cooked pasta, such as linguine.

Tepin

DRIED

PREP TIME: **10 MIN.** / TOTAL TIME: **15 MIN.** / SERVES: **8 (ABOUT 2 TABLESPOONS)**

2	cups packed fresh basil leaves (about 1 bunch)
¼	cup pine nuts
15	dried tepin chile peppers
1	garlic clove, chopped
½	cup extra-virgin olive oil
¼	cup finely grated Parmesan cheese (about 1 ounce)
½	teaspoon salt
1	lime, juiced (about 2 tablespoons juice)

1. Place basil, nuts, chiles, and garlic in a blender; process on medium speed. With blender on, gradually drizzle in oil. Add cheese, salt, and juice; process until smooth. Serve.

Calories 210; **fat calories** 170; **total fat** 20g; **sat fat** 4g; **cholesterol** 5mg; **sodium** 240mg; **total carbohydrates** 5g; **fiber** 1g; **sugars** 0g; **protein** 4g; **vitamin A IUs** 15%; **vitamin C** 6%; **calcium** 8%; **iron** 4%

Cool It Down!
Dried California chile peppers will deliver tamer heat than the tepin chiles.

MUSHROOM "RISOTTO" ,,

Emmer wheat—commonly known as farro—has similar texture to traditional risotto, but doesn't require all the stirring.

Pasilla Negro

DRIED

PREP TIME: **20 MIN.** / TOTAL TIME: **50 MIN.** / SERVES: **4**

1	6-ounce package farro
2	cups chicken broth
3	dried pasilla negro chile peppers, halved, stems and seeds removed
2	tablespoons unsalted butter
2	tablespoons extra-virgin olive oil
1	sweet onion, diced
½	teaspoon salt
¼	teaspoon freshly ground black pepper
½	pound button mushrooms, quartered (about 2 cups)
2	garlic cloves, minced
¼	cup white wine
1½	cups grated Parmesan cheese (about 6 ounces)

1. Prepare farro according to package directions, using broth instead of water and including chile.
2. Heat butter and oil in a large saucepan over medium-high heat. Add onion, salt, and black pepper; cook about 5 minutes. Add mushrooms; cook until softened, about 5 to 7 minutes. Stir in garlic. Add wine. Reduce heat; simmer until most of wine has evaporated. Stir in farro and cheese; cook until cheese is melted. Serve.

Calories 520; **fat calories** 240; **total fat** 27g; **sat fat** 14g; **cholesterol** 60mg; **sodium** 1,000mg; **total carbohydrates** 47g; **fiber** 6g; **sugars** 6g; **protein** 26g; **vitamin A IUs** 20%; **vitamin C** 8%; **calcium** 60%; **iron** 10%

RAVIOLI WITH CREAMY SPINACH PESTO 〃

Wonton wrappers can be found in the refrigerated produce section of most supermarkets. Garnish with shaved Parmesan cheese and fresh cilantro.

PREP TIME: **50 MIN.** / TOTAL TIME: **1 HR. 25 MIN.** / SERVES: **6 (4 RAVIOLI)**

Spinach Pesto
- 3 cups fresh spinach
- ¼ cup macadamia nuts
- ¼ cup whole-milk ricotta cheese
- ¼ teaspoon salt
- ¼ teaspoon black pepper
- 1 fresh yellow chile pepper, roasted, peeled, stem and seeds removed, and finely diced (about 3 tablespoons)
- ½ cup extra-virgin olive oil
- ½ cup whole milk

Ravioli
- 1 cup grated Parmesan cheese
- 1 cup whole-milk ricotta cheese
- ¼ teaspoon salt
- ¼ teaspoon black pepper
- 1 fresh yellow chile pepper, roasted, peeled, stem and seeds removed, and finely diced (about 3 tablespoons)
- 24 wonton wrappers

1. To make pesto, place spinach and next 5 ingredients in a blender or food processor; pulse until just combined. On low, slowly drizzle in oil until a smooth paste forms, about 2 minutes. Transfer to a large saucepan. Over low heat, slowly whisk in milk until mixture is creamy. Remove from heat and cover.

2. To make ravioli, line a baking sheet with parchment paper; sprinkle with flour. In a bowl, combine Parmesan cheese and next 4 ingredients (through chile). Spoon 1 tablespoon mixture onto center of wonton. Spread a line of water around border of wonton. Fold wonton in half to create a triangle. Carefully press down where edges meet; use a fork to seal edges. Repeat procedure with remaining Parmesan mixture and wontons, arranging ravioli in a single layer on prepared baking sheet.

3. Bring a large saucepan of water to a low boil. Slide 6 ravioli into boiling water. Cook, turning once, about 3 minutes. Do not let ravioli touch each other while in water. Using a slotted spoon, transfer to a plate. Repeat with remaining ravioli. Drizzle with pesto. Serve.

Calories 360; **fat calories** 255; **total fat** 29g; **sat fat** 8g; **cholesterol** 34mg; **sodium** 413mg; **total carbohydrates** 14g; **fiber** 2g; **sugars** 2g; **protein** 14g; **vitamin A IUs** 11%; **vitamin C** 45%; **calcium** 30%; **iron** 8%

VEGGIE ORZO 🌶

Rice-shaped orzo pasta is a perfect vehicle for colorful sweet peppers and summer vegetables.

Cherry Bell
FRESH

Bell Pepper
FRESH

PREP TIME: **20 MIN.** / TOTAL TIME: **40 MIN.** / SERVES: **6 (ABOUT 2 CUPS)**

- 1 16-ounce package orzo pasta
- 2 tablespoons unsalted butter
- 2 tablespoons extra-virgin olive oil
- 1 small sweet onion, finely diced (about ½ cup)
- 2 bunches baby broccoli, trimmed and chopped (about 1 pound)
- 6 fresh cherry bell chile peppers, stems and seeds removed, sliced into thin rounds (about ½ pound)
- 1 fresh red bell pepper, stem and seeds removed, diced (about ½ cup)
- 1 fresh yellow bell pepper, stem and seeds removed, diced (about ½ cup)
- 2 garlic cloves, minced
- 1½ cups crumbled feta cheese (about 6 ounces)

Salt

Freshly ground black pepper

1. Prepare orzo according to package directions. Drain.

2. Heat butter and oil in a large saucepan over medium-high heat. Add onion and broccoli; cook until onion is translucent, stirring occasionally, about 3 to 5 minutes. Add chile, peppers, and garlic; cook until vegetables are slightly tender, about 5 minutes.

3. In a bowl, combine orzo, feta, and cooked vegetables; add salt and black pepper to taste. Toss together. Serve.

Calories 490; **fat calories** 160; **total fat** 18g; **sat fat** 9g; **cholesterol** 45mg; **sodium** 450mg; **total carbohydrates** 67g; **fiber** 5g; **sugars** 6g; **protein** 19g; **vitamin A IUs** 50%; **vitamin C** 320%; **calcium** 25%; **iron** 20%

Heat It Up!
Try fresh red Fresno chiles for a punch of spice.

RASPBERRY-CHILE CHICKEN THIGHS 〃

If Hatch chiles are not in season, substitute banana wax chile peppers.

FRESH

PREP TIME: **20 MIN.** / TOTAL TIME: **1 HR. 50 MIN.** / SERVES: **6 (2 THIGHS)**

- 12 chicken thighs (about 5 pounds)
- ½ teaspoon salt
- 2 tablespoons extra-virgin olive oil
- 2 tablespoons unsalted butter
- 2 cups seedless raspberry preserves
- 3 tablespoons red wine vinegar
- 4 fresh Hatch chile peppers, roasted, peeled, stems and seeds removed, and diced
- 2 lemons, juiced (about 6 tablespoons juice)
- 1 tablespoon smoked paprika
- 1 tablespoon cayenne pepper

1. Sprinkle chicken evenly with salt. Heat oil and butter in a large flameproof roasting pan over medium-high heat. Add 6 pieces chicken; sear, about 5 minutes per side. Remove from pan and add remaining 6 pieces chicken; repeat procedure. Return all chicken to roasting pan.

2. Preheat oven to 350°F. In a small saucepan over medium heat, combine preserves, vinegar, chile, and juice; cook just until boiling, stirring occasionally. Reduce heat; simmer until slightly thickened, stirring constantly, about 5 minutes. Cool slightly.

3. Place preserves mixture in a blender*; process until slightly smooth. Pour preserves mixture over chicken; sprinkle evenly with paprika and cayenne pepper. Cover with foil; bake at 350°F for 45 minutes. Uncover; bake until chicken is completely cooked through and a meat thermometer inserted into thickest part reads 165°F, about 15 minutes. Serve.

*Note: Be cautious when blending hot foods; the contents expand rapidly, causing a risk of scalding. To be safe, before blending, remove center piece of blender lid (to allow steam to escape), secure lid on blender, and place a towel over opening in lid (to avoid splatters).

Calories 740; **fat calories** 240; **total fat** 26g; **sat fat** 8g; **cholesterol** 300mg; **sodium** 390mg; **total carbohydrates** 73g; **fiber** 1g; **sugars** 65g; **protein** 53g; **vitamin A IUs** 25%; **vitamin C** 90%; **calcium** 2%; **iron** 15%

Kitchen Savvy

If your roasting pan isn't stove-top safe, sear chicken in a large skillet, in batches if necessary, before transferring to the roasting pan.

Cherry Bell

FRESH

CHICKEN AND CHERRY BELL CHOW MEIN 🌶

Chow mein is an American term for a dish containing stir-fried noodles.

PREP TIME: **1 HR.** / TOTAL TIME: **2 HR. 40 MIN.** / SERVES: **8 (ABOUT 2½ CUPS)**

Heat It Up!

Want some heat? Pop the stems off a couple of dried de arbol chile peppers and toss the chiles in during the stir-fry step.

½ cup soy sauce, divided
3 tablespoons hoisin sauce, divided
3 teaspoons oyster sauce, divided
½ teaspoon chili oil
½ teaspoon toasted sesame oil
¾ pound skinless, boneless chicken thighs
1 pound dried chow mein noodles
3 tablespoons peanut oil, divided
1 tablespoon unsalted butter
¼ pound button mushrooms, quartered (about 1 cup)
3 garlic cloves, minced
4 green onions, trimmed and sliced diagonally
½ pound fresh cherry bell chile peppers, stem and seeds removed, thinly sliced
¼ pound sugar snap peas, strings removed, halved crosswise
Salt
Freshly ground black pepper

1. In a large bowl, combine ¼ cup soy sauce, 1 tablespoon hoisin sauce, 1 teaspoon oyster sauce, and chili and sesame oils; add chicken. Cover bowl with plastic wrap; place bowl in refrigerator. Let sit, stirring often, 1 hour.
2. Prepare noodles according to package directions. Rinse with cold water; drain.
3. Preheat oven to 350°F. Heat 1 tablespoon peanut oil and butter in a large wok or ovenproof skillet. Add chicken; cook 2 minutes per side. Transfer to oven; bake at 350°F until chicken is completely cooked through and a meat thermometer inserted into thickest part reads 165°F, about 15 minutes. Cool chicken until can be handled. Shred chicken.
4. Heat remaining 2 tablespoons peanut oil in a wok or large skillet over high heat. Add mushrooms; cook, stirring occasionally, 2 minutes. Add garlic. Add remaining ¼ cup soy sauce, remaining 2 tablespoons hoisin sauce, remaining 2 teaspoons oyster sauce, noodles, green onions, cherry bell chile peppers, and sugar snap peas; cook, stirring constantly, until vegetables are crisp-tender. Add shredded chicken to pan; cook until heated through. Stir in salt and black pepper to taste. Serve.

Calories 350; **fat calories** 100; **total fat** 11g; **sat fat** 3g; **cholesterol** 30mg; **sodium** 1,350mg; **total carbohydrates** 48g; **fiber** 5g; **sugars** 5g; **protein** 16g; **vitamin A IUs** 25%; **vitamin C** 70%; **calcium** 2%; **iron** 15%

CHICKEN FRIED RICE 〃

For more flavor and some color, stir in ½ cup of diced red bell pepper.

PREP TIME: **20 MIN.** / TOTAL TIME: **30 MIN.** / SERVES: **4 (ABOUT 1¼ CUPS)**

Japones

||||||||||||||||||||

DRIED

||||||||||||||||||||

- 1 tablespoon unsalted butter
- 1 tablespoon extra-virgin olive oil
- 1 onion, chopped (about ⅔ cup)
- 4 dried japones chile peppers, stems and seeds removed
- 2 garlic cloves, minced
- 2 large eggs, beaten
- 1½ cups cooked rice
- ½ cup diced cooked chicken breast
- ¼ cup chopped proscuitto
- ½ teaspoon salt
- ¼ teaspoon ground cayenne pepper
- 1 green onion, diagonally sliced

1. Heat butter and oil in a wok or large skillet over medium-high heat. Add onion, chiles, and garlic; cook until onion is translucent, stirring occasionally, about 3 minutes. Push onion mixture to one side of pan. Add eggs to other side and scramble. Combine eggs and onion mixture; toss together.
2. Stir in rice and remaining ingredients; cook until chicken is heated through, stirring occasionally, about 5 minutes. Serve.

Calories 280; **fat calories** 120; **total fat** 14g; **sat fat** 4g; **cholesterol** 130mg; **sodium** 660mg; **total carbohydrates** 24g; **fiber** 1g; **sugars** 2g; **protein** 14g; **vitamin A IUs** 12%; **vitamin C** 8%; **calcium** 4%; **iron** 4%

Heat It Up!
The daring can substitute ground dried bhut jolokia for the japones, but be sure to only use ¼ teaspoon since it's extremely hot.

POLLO EN CREMA „

Serve over hot cooked rice or wide egg noodles; garnish with fresh chopped cilantro, if desired.

PREP TIME: **20 MIN.** / TOTAL TIME: **55 MIN.** / SERVES: **6**

- 4 pounds bone-in, skin-on chicken pieces, trimmed
- 3 garlic cloves, thinly sliced
- 3 dried chipotle chile peppers, stems and seeds removed
- 1 cup sour cream
- ⅛ teaspoon salt
- 2 tablespoons extra-virgin olive oil
- 1 small sweet onion, thinly sliced (about ⅔ cup)
- 2 large Roma tomatoes, finely chopped (about ¾ cup)

1. In a large, straight-sided sauté pan, sear chicken skin side down in a single layer over medium-high heat, about 3 minutes. Sprinkle evenly with garlic; add chiles and water to cover. Bring just to boiling. Reduce heat; simmer until chicken is completely cooked through and a meat thermometer inserted into thickest part reads 165°F, about 20 to 25 minutes. Transfer chicken to a plate, reserving chiles and liquid. Place chiles and 2 cups liquid from sauté pan in a blender*, discarding any remaining liquid; add sour cream and salt. Process until smooth. **2.** Return empty sauté pan to stovetop. Add oil; heat over medium-high heat. Add onion and tomato; cook, stirring

occasionally, 3 minutes. Add chile mixture; bring just to boiling. Nestle chicken into chile mixture; simmer until chicken is heated through, about 5 minutes. Serve.

Note: *Be cautious when blending hot foods; the contents expand rapidly, causing a risk of scalding. To be safe, before blending, remove center piece of blender lid (to allow steam to escape), secure lid on blender, and place a towel over opening in lid (to avoid splatters).*

Calories 500; **fat calories** 290; **total fat** 32g; **sat fat** 11g; **cholesterol** 175mg; **sodium** 130mg; **total carbohydrates** 9g; **fiber** 1g; **sugars** 3g; **protein** 40g; **vitamin A IUs** 35%; **vitamin C** 10%; **calcium** 6%; **iron** 15%

Red Savina Habanero

FRESH

Make Ahead

Assemble the enchiladas in the baking dish the night before; cover and refrigerate. Bake an additional 15 minutes.

CHICKEN ENCHILADAS 〉〉〉

In addition to chicken, these classic enchiladas work well with thinly sliced beef rump roast, shredded pork, or even shredded turkey.

PREP TIME: **45 MIN.** / TOTAL TIME: **2 HR. 25 MIN.** / SERVES: **6 (2 ENCHILADAS)**

- 2 tablespoons unsalted butter
- 1 onion, thinly sliced (about 1½ cups)
- 6 cups chicken broth
- 1 tablespoon ground cumin
- 1 tablespoon dried oregano, crushed
- 1 teaspoon salt
- 2 14.5-ounce cans fire-roasted or stewed tomatoes, drained
- 1 fresh red Savina habanero chile pepper, stem and seeds removed, split lengthwise
- 2 pounds skinless, boneless chicken breasts
- 12 6-inch corn tortillas
- 3½ cups shredded cheddar cheese (about 14 ounces)

Diced tomatoes (optional)
Shredded lettuce (optional)
Sliced avocado (optional)

1. In a straight-sided sauté pan, melt butter over medium-high heat. Add onion; cook until softened, stirring often, about 7 to 10 minutes. Stir in broth and next 5 ingredients (through chile); bring just to boiling. Reduce heat; simmer 15 minutes.

2. Using an immersion blender, carefully blend sauce until smooth. Add chicken to sauté pan; bring onion mixture to a boil. Simmer until chicken is completely cooked through and a meat thermometer inserted into thickest part reads 165°F, about 30 minutes. Remove chicken; cool until can be handled. Shred chicken.

3. Preheat oven to 350°F. Coat bottom of a 9 x 13–inch baking dish with thin layer of blended sauce. Dip each tortilla in remaining sauce; fill tortillas evenly with chicken and cheese, using only 1½ cups cheese. Roll filled tortillas as you prepare, arranging seam side down and side by side in prepared baking dish.

4. Top enchiladas with remaining sauce and remaining 2 cups cheese. Bake at 350°F until cheese is melted and enchiladas are heated through, about 15 minutes. Top with tomato, lettuce, and avocado, if desired. Serve.

Calories 670; **fat calories** 260; **total fat** 29g; **sat fat** 16g; **cholesterol** 80mg; **sodium** 1,140mg; **total carbohydrates** 41g; **fiber** 6g; **sugars** 9g; **protein** 59g; **vitamin A IUs** 25%; **vitamin C** 30%; **calcium** 50%; **iron** 8%

LETTUCE-WRAPPED TACOS ""

East meets West in this fusion of Vietnamese-style lettuce wraps and tacos.

Serrano

FRESH

PREP TIME: **35 MIN.** / TOTAL TIME: **8 HR. 40 MIN.** / SERVES: **8 (ABOUT 1¼ CUPS)**

¾   cup packed brown sugar
½   cup soy sauce
½   cup extra-virgin olive oil
1   tablespoon dry mustard
2   tablespoons Worcestershire sauce
8   garlic cloves, minced (about ½ cup), divided
4   fresh serrano chile peppers, stems and seeds removed, finely diced (about 3 tablespoons), divided
1¼ cups lime juice, divided (about 8 limes)
1½ pounds beef tri-tip
Vegetable oil
1½ cups fresh cilantro leaves, chopped
6   green onions, trimmed and sliced
4   Roma tomatoes, diced
1   red onion, sliced (about 1 cup)
8   butter lettuce leaves
2   cups shredded cheddar cheese (about 8 ounces, optional)

1. In a bowl, whisk together brown sugar, soy sauce, oil, mustard, Worcestershire sauce, half of garlic, half of chile, and 1 cup juice. In a large zip-top plastic bag, combine beef and brown sugar mixture. Seal bag; turn bag several times to mix well and coat beef. Refrigerate 8 hours or overnight.

2. Preheat grill to medium-high heat. Oil grill rack. Remove beef from zip-top plastic bag; discard marinade. Place beef on grill rack; grill until both sides are marked, about 3 to 5 minutes per side. Turn off all but one burner; move beef to cool side of grill rack and partially cover. Grill until desired doneness (125°F for rare, 135°F for medium, or 145°F for well done), about 15 to 25 minutes. Let meat rest 15 minutes. Slice thinly against the grain.

3. In a bowl, combine remaining half of garlic, remaining half of chile, remaining ¼ cup juice, cilantro, green onions, tomato, and onion.

4. Top lettuce leaves evenly with beef and chile mixture. Sprinkle evenly with cheese, if desired. Serve.

Calories 520; **fat calories** 290; **total fat** 32g; **sat fat** 11g; **cholesterol** 90mg; **sodium** 1,070mg; **total carbohydrates** 31g; **fiber** 3g; **sugars** 19g; **protein** 30g; **vitamin A IUs** 70%; **vitamin C** 70%; **calcium** 30%; **iron** 20%

Simple Swap

Tri-tip comes from the bottom side of the sirloin and can sometimes be hard to find; you can easily substitute beef tenderloin.

CASCABEL KETCHUP-TOPPED MEAT LOAF 〉〉

Cascabel

DRIED

This recipe makes plenty of ketchup, perfect for spicing up French fries or topping your next burger.

PREP TIME: **1 HR.** / TOTAL TIME: **2 HR. 30 MIN.** / SERVES: **6 (1 SLICE)**

Ketchup

- 1 1-ounce package dried Cascabel chile peppers, stems and seeds removed
- 1 tablespoon extra-virgin olive oil
- 1 onion, diced (about 1 cup)
- ½ cup cider vinegar
- 3 tablespoons brown sugar
- 2 garlic cloves, minced
- 1 teaspoon Worcestershire sauce
- ½ teaspoon salt
- ½ teaspoon dry mustard
- ⅛ teaspoon ground allspice
- ⅛ teaspoon ground cinnamon
- ⅛ teaspoon ground cloves
- ⅛ teaspoon ground cumin
- 1 28-ounce can whole tomatoes, drained

Meat Loaf

- 1 tablespoon extra-virgin olive oil
- 1 onion, diced (about 1 cup)
- 1 carrot, finely chopped
- 3 garlic cloves, minced
- 1 pound lean ground beef
- 1 pound bulk Italian sausage
- ¾ cup Italian breadcrumbs
- ¼ cup barbecue sauce
- 1 large egg, beaten slightly
- 1 teaspoon smoked paprika
- ½ teaspoon salt
- ¼ teaspoon freshly ground black pepper

1. To make ketchup, in a bowl, combine chiles and sufficient hot water to cover; let sit until plump, stirring occasionally, about 15 to 30 minutes. Discard soaking liquid.

2. Heat oil in a large saucepan over medium heat. Add onion; cook until softened, stirring once, about 10 to 12 minutes. Place chiles, onion, vinegar, and remaining ketchup ingredients in a blender*; process until smooth. Return chile mixture to saucepan. Simmer for 20 minutes.

3. To make meat loaf, heat oil in a medium skillet over medium heat. Add onion; cook until softened, stirring occasionally, about 10 to 12 minutes. Add carrot and garlic; cook until carrot softens, 5 minutes. Cool 10 minutes.

4. Preheat oven to 350°F. Lightly coat a baking dish with cooking spray. In a bowl, combine onion mixture, beef, and remaining meat loaf ingredients. Form meat mixture into a tall, rectangular loaf, about 10 x 4 inches; place in prepared baking dish. Bake at 350°F for 15 minutes. Top with ½ cup ketchup. Bake until a meat thermometer inserted into center of loaf reads 155°F, about 1 to 1¼ hours. Let rest 10 minutes. Serve with remaining ketchup.

*Note: Be cautious when blending hot foods; the contents expand rapidly, causing a risk of scalding. To be safe, before blending, remove center piece of blender lid (to allow steam to escape), secure lid on blender, and place a towel over opening in lid (to avoid splatters).

Calories 560; **fat calories** 290; **total fat** 32g; **sat fat** 10g; **cholesterol** 135mg; **sodium** 1,410mg; **total carbohydrates** 37g; **fiber** 4g; **sugars** 10g; **protein** 30g; **vitamin A IUs** 190%; **vitamin C** 35%; **calcium** 10%; **iron** 15%

Savina Ruby Hot

DRIED

Bell Pepper

FRESH

SMOKY CHIPPED BEEF ON TOAST 🌶🌶🌶

Here's an updated version of a classic Army dish that predates World War I. Purchase smoked brisket at your local barbecue joint.

PREP TIME: **15 MIN.** / TOTAL TIME: **35 MIN.** / SERVES: **6**

Simple Swap

Substitute home-style white bread if you can't find buttermilk bread.

- 1 tablespoon extra-virgin olive oil
- 1 tablespoon unsalted butter
- ½ onion, finely diced (about ⅓ cup)
- 1 garlic clove, minced
- ½ dried Savina Ruby Hot habanero chile pepper, stem and seeds removed
- ¼ cup all-purpose flour
- 2 cups whole milk
- 1 teaspoon smoked paprika
- 1 fresh red bell pepper, stem and seeds removed, diced (about ½ cup)
- ¾ pound smoked brisket, chopped

Salt

Freshly ground black pepper

- 6 slices buttermilk bread, toasted

1. Heat oil and butter in a large saucepan over medium heat until butter is melted completely. Add onion, garlic, and chile; cook until onion is softened, stirring occasionally, about 3 to 5 minutes. Add flour; cook, stirring constantly, 1 minute. Slowly whisk in milk and paprika. Add bell pepper; bring just to boiling. Reduce heat; simmer until thickened, stirring occasionally, about 4 to 5 minutes. Add beef; stir in salt and black pepper to taste. Cook until beef is heated through, stirring occasionally, about 8 to 10 minutes. Spoon beef mixture over bread slices. Serve.

Calories 394; **fat calories** 184; **total fat** 20g; **sat fat** 7g; **cholesterol** 69mg; **sodium** 795mg; **total carbohydrates** 36g; **fiber** 3g; **sugars** 11g; **protein** 1g; **vitamin A IUs** 40%; **vitamin C** 70%; **calcium** 25%; **iron** 15%

STEAK BRACIOLE AND POACHED EGGS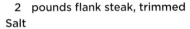

Trinidad Scorpion

DRIED

Braciole is a Sicilian dish of filled and rolled slices of meat.

PREP TIME: **25 MIN.** / TOTAL TIME: **1 HR.** / SERVES: **8**

2 pounds flank steak, trimmed
Salt
Freshly ground black pepper
1 portobello mushroom, stem and gills removed, sliced
8 ounces sliced mozzarella cheese
¼ cup extra-virgin olive oil, divided
3½ cups beef broth, divided
2 tablespoons unsalted butter
2 shallots, finely diced (about ¼ cup)
2 garlic cloves, minced
½ dried Trinidad scorpion chile pepper, stem and seeds removed
¼ cup sherry
1 pound button mushrooms, quartered
½ cup heavy cream
2 tablespoons cornstarch
3 tablespoons cold water
1 tablespoon white wine vinegar
8 large eggs

1. Preheat oven to 350°F. Pound flank steak with a meat mallet to between ⅛ and ¼ inch thick. Sprinkle evenly with ½ teaspoon salt and ¼ teaspoon black pepper. Top with portobello slices and cheese. Roll up steak, jelly-roll style, and secure with butcher's twine or seal with toothpicks.
2. Heat 2 tablespoons oil in a large, oven-safe skillet. Add steak; sear on all sides. Add 1½ cups broth. Bake at 350°F until a meat thermometer inserted into center reads 140°F, about 15 to 30 minutes.
3. Heat remaining 2 tablespoons oil and butter in a small saucepan over medium-high heat. Add shallot; cook, stirring occasionally, about 3 to 5 minutes. Add garlic, chile, and sherry; cook 1 minute. Add remaining 2 cups beef broth, button mushrooms, and cream. Reduce heat; simmer until slightly thickened, stirring often, about 5 to 6 minutes.
4. In a bowl, whisk together cornstarch and 3 tablespoons cold water until smooth; stir into shallot mixture. Simmer until thickened, about 4 to 5 minutes. Discard chile; stir in salt and black pepper to taste.
5. Fill a large, straight-sided sauté pan with water to 1 inch from the top. Stir in 1 teaspoon salt and vinegar; bring to a simmer. Crack eggs, one at a time, into a small bowl or cup; gently lower into simmering water. (You can poach 2 to 3 eggs at a time.) After you drop the last egg,
turn off heat; cover pan. Cook until egg whites are firm but yolk is runny, about 3 to 5 minutes. Remove poached eggs with a slotted spoon; transfer to a paper towel–lined plate. Repeat with remaining eggs.
6. Cut steak roll into 8 slices; top each slice evenly with a poached egg and shallot-cream mixture. Serve.

Calories 510; fat calories 310; **total fat** 35g; **sat fat** 15g; **cholesterol** 275mg; **sodium** 690mg; **total carbohydrates** 8g; **fiber** 1g; **sugars** 2g; **protein** 37g; **vitamin A IUs** 15%; **vitamin C** 2%; **calcium** 25%; **iron** 20%

BEEF BARBACOA 〃

Serve this hearty dish with corn tortillas, sliced red onion, and cilantro.

PREP TIME: **30 MIN.** / TOTAL TIME: **2 HR. 50 MIN.** / SERVES: **8 (ABOUT 2¼ CUPS)**

Hatch

DRIED

Poblano

FRESH

Bell Pepper

FRESH

- 4 dried Hatch chile peppers, stems and seeds removed
- 2 garlic cloves, minced
- 1 teaspoon dried oregano, crushed
- 2 tablespoons extra-virgin olive oil
- 2 pounds stew meat (beef chuck or pork shoulder), cut into 1-inch pieces
- ½ cup sliced green olives
- ½ teaspoon ground cumin
- ½ tablespoon salt
- 2 tomatoes, chopped (about 2 cups)
- 1 large fresh poblano chile pepper, stem and seeds removed, finely chopped
- 1 large fresh green bell pepper, stem and seeds removed, chopped (about 1 cup)
- 1 small white onion, finely chopped (about ⅔ cup)
- 1 12-ounce can or bottle dark beer
- 1 teaspoon freshly ground black pepper

1. In a large saucepan, combine Hatch chiles and enough water to cover; bring just to boiling. Reduce heat; simmer until Hatch chiles are softened, about 5 minutes. Let cool. Drain chiles over a bowl, retaining 1 cup chile water; discard remaining chile water.
2. Place chiles, 1 cup chile water, garlic, and oregano in a food processor or blender*; pulse until smooth.
3. Heat oil in a large saucepan over medium-high heat. Add stew meat; cook until browned, stirring occasionally, about 10 minutes. Stir in Hatch chile mixture, olives, and remaining ingredients. Bring just to boiling. Reduce heat to lowest setting and cover; simmer until meat is very tender, stirring occasionally, about 2 hours. Serve.

*Note: Be cautious when blending hot foods; the contents expand rapidly, causing a risk of scalding. To be safe, before blending, remove center piece of blender lid (to allow steam to escape), secure lid on blender, and place a towel over opening in lid (to avoid splatters).

Calories 230; **fat calories** 90; **total fat** 10g; **sat fat** 2.5g; **cholesterol** 75mg; **sodium** 600mg; **total carbohydrates** 9g; **fiber** 2g; **sugars** 2g; **protein** 26g; **vitamin A IUs** 10%; **vitamin C** 45%; **calcium** 4%; **iron** 15%

SAVINA MASHED POTATO-STUFFED RIB EYES 🌶🌶🌶

You will not use all the mashed potatoes; serve with steaks or reserve for another use.

PREP TIME: **45 MIN.** / TOTAL TIME: **1 HR. 20 MIN.** / SERVES: **6 (1 STUFFED RIB EYE)**

Cool It Down!

Swap out the red Savina habanero for a fresh cayenne chile pepper to relieve the heat.

6 Yukon gold potatoes, peeled and quartered (about 4 pounds)

3 turnips, peeled and quartered (about 1½ pounds)

1 fresh red Savina habanero chile pepper, stem and seeds removed

Salt

½ cup sour cream

4 tablespoons unsalted butter, softened (¼ cup)

3 garlic cloves, minced

Vegetable oil

6 8-ounce thick-cut rib eye steaks

12 short bamboo skewers, soaked in water for 30 minutes

1. In a large stockpot, combine potato, turnip, and Savina chile; add just enough cold water to cover. Bring to a low boil; stir in 1 tablespoon salt. Cook until fork tender, about 20 minutes; drain and return potato and turnip to stockpot. Add sour cream, butter, and garlic; mash until smooth. Cool.

2. Preheat grill to medium-high heat. Oil grill rack. Using a sharp knife, create a pocket in the side of each steak. Fill each pocket with potato mixture. Seal stuffed steaks with skewers; sprinkle with salt. Place steaks on grill rack; grill until desired doneness (125°F for rare, 135°F for medium, or 145°F for well done), about 6 to 10 minutes per side. Serve.

Calories 1,080; **fat calories** 620; **total fat** 68g; **sat fat** 32g; **cholesterol** 210mg; **sodium** 1,410mg; **total carbohydrates** 62g; **fiber** 6g; **sugars** 5g; **protein** 49g; **vitamin A IUs** 15%; **vitamin C** 150%; **calcium** 8%; **iron** 40%

BACON-WRAPPED STUFFED ANAHEIM CHILES ◗

Anaheim

FRESH

Round out your meal by serving these stuffed chiles with Spanish rice.

PREP TIME: **50 MIN.** / TOTAL TIME: **1 HR. 15 MIN.** / SERVES: **16 (1 STUFFED CHILE)**

16 slices bacon (about 1 pound)
16 large fresh Anaheim chile peppers (about 2 pounds)
2 cups shredded pepper-Jack cheese (about 8 ounces)
1 cup sliced pepperoncini peppers
½ cup oil-packed sun-dried tomatoes, drained and chopped
1 14-ounce can sliced black olives, drained (about ¾ cup)

1. Arrange bacon slices in a single layer on a baking sheet and broil under a low broiler until bacon is partially cooked but still pliable, about 5 to 8 minutes. Transfer to paper towels to drain; cool.

2. Preheat oven to 350°F. Line a baking sheet with foil. Make a lengthwise cut along the side of each Anaheim chile; carefully remove seeds, leaving stem intact. In a bowl, combine cheese, pepperoncini pepper, sun-dried tomato, and olives. Spoon cheese mixture evenly into chiles; wrap each chile with a bacon slice, securing with toothpicks. Arrange on prepared baking sheet. Bake at 350°F until bacon is completely cooked and cheese is melted, turning once, about 20 minutes. Serve.

Calories 240; **fat calories** 170; **total fat** 19g; **sat fat** 7g; **cholesterol** 40mg; **sodium** 690mg; **total carbohydrates** 9g; **fiber** 2g; **sugars** 4g; **protein** 12g; **vitamin A IUs** 20%; **vitamin C** 120%; **calcium** 10%; **iron** 2%

SPICY PORK STIR-FRY "

Yakisoba noodles are similar to ramen noodles.

PREP TIME: **35 MIN.** / TOTAL TIME: **1 HR. 25 MIN.** / SERVES: **6 (ABOUT 2½ CUPS)**

De Arbol

DRIED

Bell Pepper

FRESH

¾ cup soy sauce, divided

4 garlic cloves, minced, divided

2 tablespoons cornstarch, divided

1 pound pork tenderloin, cut into 2-inch strips

1 16-ounce package yakisoba noodles

¾ cup sweet chili sauce

1 tablespoon granulated garlic

1 ½-inch piece fresh ginger, peeled and minced (about 1 tablespoon)

3 tablespoons peanut oil

1 large sweet onion, thinly sliced (about 2 cups)

1 dried de arbol chile pepper, stem and seeds removed

2 carrots, thinly sliced or shaved

2 fresh green onions, ends trimmed, diagonally cut

1 fresh red bell pepper, stem and seeds removed, thinly sliced

1 fresh yellow bell pepper, stem and seeds removed, thinly sliced

1 fresh green bell pepper, stem and seeds removed, thinly sliced

½ cup cold water

1 pound napa cabbage, shredded (about 5 cups)

1. In a bowl, combine ½ cup soy sauce, half of garlic, and 1 tablespoon cornstarch. Add pork; toss together. Cover bowl with plastic wrap. Let sit 30 minutes. Remove pork; discard marinade.

2. Prepare noodles according to package directions; drain and rinse noodles in cool water; drain.

3. In a large bowl, combine remaining ¼ cup soy sauce, chili sauce, granulated garlic, and ginger. Add noodles; toss together.

4. Heat oil in a wok or large skillet over medium-high heat. Add sweet onion; cook, stirring occasionally, 3 minutes. Add remaining half of garlic and chile; cook 2 minutes. Add pork; cook, stirring constantly, 2 minutes. Add carrot, green onions, and bell peppers; cook until pork is completely cooked through, about 6 minutes.

5. In a bowl, stir remaining 1 tablespoon cornstarch into ½ cup cold water until smooth; add to pork mixture. Cook, stirring, 2 minutes. Add shredded cabbage; toss together. Fluff noodles with a fork; spoon pork mixture on top. Serve.

Calories 430; **fat calories** 110; **total fat** 12g; **sat fat** 2.5g; **cholesterol** 55mg; **sodium** 1,840mg; **total carbohydrates** 57g; **fiber** 7g; **sugars** 17g; **protein** 25g; **vitamin A IUs** 250%; **vitamin C** 210%; **calcium** 10%; **iron** 10%

SLOW-COOKED STOVE-TOP PORK ROAST "

Perfect for tacos or tostadas—serve with fresh salsa, avocado slices, red onion, sour cream, and cilantro.

PREP TIME: **30 MIN.** / TOTAL TIME: **3 HR. 50 MIN.** / SERVES: **12 (1 CUP PORK)**

Pasilla Negro

DRIED

New Mexico

DRIED

De Arbol

DRIED

- 3 dried pasilla negro chile peppers, stems and seeds removed
- 5 dried New Mexico chile peppers, stems and seeds removed
- 5 dried de arbol chile peppers, stems and seeds removed
- 1 tablespoon canola oil
- ¼ onion, thinly sliced (about ¼ cup)
- 2 garlic cloves, coarsely chopped
- ½ cup beef broth
- 1 teaspoon lemon juice
- 4 teaspoons ground cayenne
- 2 teaspoons chili powder
- 1 teaspoon salt
- ½ teaspoon ground cumin
- 6 pounds bone-in pork butt roast

1. Bring 6 cups water just to boiling in a large saucepan. Add dried chiles; cook, stirring often, 5 minutes. Drain chiles over a bowl; discard 2 cups chile water. Retain remaining water and chiles.
2. Heat oil in a large straight-sided sauté pan over medium-high heat. Add onion and garlic; cook, stirring often, 5 minutes.
3. In a large bowl, combine chiles and their water, onion mixture,

broth and next 5 ingredients (through cumin).
4. Place half of chile mixture in a blender*; process until smooth. Repeat procedure with remaining chile mixture.
5. Heat a Dutch oven over high heat. Add pork, fat side down; cook until browned, turning several times, about 10 minutes. Stir in chile mixture; bring just to boiling. Reduce heat and partially cover; simmer until pork easily pulls apart with a fork, about 3 to 4 hours.
6. Remove pork; cool until can be handled, about 30 minutes. Shred pork. Serve.

*****Note:** Be cautious when blending hot foods; the contents expand rapidly, causing a risk of scalding. To be safe, before blending, remove center piece of blender lid (to allow steam to escape), secure lid on blender, and place a towel over opening in lid (to avoid splatters).*

Calories 160; **fat calories** 60; **total fat** 7g; **sat fat** 2g; **cholesterol** 60mg; **sodium** 590mg; **total carbohydrates** 5g; **fiber** 0g; **sugars** 0g; **protein** 9g; **vitamin A IUs** 10%; **vitamin C** 2%; **calcium** 2%; **iron** 8%

HASSELBACK RED POTATOES WITH CHILE-BASIL CREAM

side dishes

Yellow

FRESH

HASSELBACK RED POTATOES WITH CHILE-BASIL CREAM ⟩

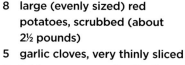

Place a wooden chopstick along each side of the potato to prevent your knife from cutting all the way through.

PREP TIME: **20 MIN.** / TOTAL TIME: **55 MIN.** / SERVES: **8 (1 POTATO)**

8   large (evenly sized) red potatoes, scrubbed (about 2½ pounds)
5   garlic cloves, very thinly sliced
3   tablespoons unsalted butter, melted
3   tablespoons extra-virgin olive oil
Salt
Freshly ground black pepper
1   cup sour cream
2   fresh yellow chile peppers, charred, peeled, stems and seeds removed, finely diced
¼   ounce fresh basil leaves, finely diced
Fresh basil leaves (optional)

1. Preheat oven to 425°F. Line a baking sheet with foil. Partially slice potatoes crosswise in thin slices, taking care not to cut completely through bottom (making a fan).
2. Place garlic slices evenly between potato slices. In a bowl, whisk together butter and oil; brush evenly over potatoes. Sprinkle with salt and black pepper. Arrange on prepared baking sheet. Bake at 425°F until potatoes are golden brown and cooked through, about 25 to 30 minutes.
3. In a bowl, combine sour cream, chile, and basil; top potatoes evenly with chile mixture. Garnish with basil leaves. Serve.

Calories 250; **fat calories** 130; **total fat** 14g; **sat fat** 7g; **cholesterol** 30mg; **sodium** 35mg; **total carbohydrates** 25g; **fiber** 3g; **sugars** 3g; **protein** 4g; **vitamin A IUs** 10%; **vitamin C** 70%; **calcium** 4%; **iron** 8%

CHILE-ROASTED SPUDS 🌶🌶

Add extra flavor to this summer side by tossing in chopped fresh herbs, such as basil or rosemary, just before serving.

Bell Pepper
FRESH

Cayenne
FRESH

PREP TIME: **20 MIN.** / TOTAL TIME: **32 MIN.** / SERVES: **8 (ABOUT 2 CUPS)**

1½ pounds Dutch yellow potatoes, quartered

8 cipolline onions, peeled (about ¾ pound)

1 large fresh red bell pepper, halved, stem and seeds removed

2 fresh cayenne chile peppers, stems and seeds removed

3 garlic cloves, peeled

2 tablespoons extra-virgin olive oil

Salt

1. Preheat oven to 425°F. Line a baking sheet with foil. In a bowl, combine potato and next 5 ingredients (through oil); toss together. Sprinkle with salt. Arrange in an even layer on prepared baking sheet. Bake at 425°F until slightly charred, about 12 to 15 minutes. Cool until can be handled, about 10 minutes.

2. Chop onions, bell peppers, chiles, and garlic. Return to potatoes; gently toss together. Serve.

Calories 150; **fat calories** 45; **total fat** 5g; **sat fat** 0.5g; **cholesterol** 0mg; **sodium** 25mg; **total carbohydrates** 24g; **fiber** 4g; **sugars** 5g; **protein** 3g; **vitamin A IUs** 25%; **vitamin C** 110%; **calcium** 2%; **iron** 6%

Heat It Up!

Swap out the cayenne chile peppers for fresh red Savina habanero chile peppers if you're feeling daring.

POTATO, TURNIP, AND SWEET PEPPER AU GRATIN

Veggie Sweet Mini

FRESH

Serve this cheesy dish at your next holiday meal.

PREP TIME: **30 MIN.** / TOTAL TIME: **2 HR. 12 MIN.** / SERVES: **12 (ABOUT 1½ CUPS)**

- 4 tablespoons unsalted butter, divided (¼ cup)
- 3 tablespoons all-purpose flour
- 3 cups whole milk
- Salt
- Freshly ground white pepper
- 1 tablespoon extra-virgin olive oil
- 1 pound fresh veggie sweet mini peppers, stems and seeds removed, sliced into rounds
- 1½ pounds Yukon gold potatoes, peeled and thinly sliced
- 1 pound turnips, peeled and thinly sliced
- 4½ cups shredded sharp cheddar cheese, divided (about 18 ounces)

1. Heat 3 tablespoons butter in a medium saucepan over medium heat. Add flour; cook until golden, stirring often, 2 to 3 minutes. Thoroughly whisk in milk. Simmer until sauce coats the back of a spoon, stirring often (do not let mixture burn), about 20 minutes. Stir in salt and pepper to taste.
2. In a small skillet, heat remaining 1 tablespoon butter and oil over medium-high heat. Add mini peppers; cook until slightly softened, about 5 minutes. Cool.
3. Preheat oven to 350°F. Spread ¼ cup sauce on bottom of a 13 x 9–inch baking dish. Add a layer of mini peppers, potatoes, and turnips. Sprinkle with cheese to cover; drizzle with sauce. Repeat layering, using all remaining ingredients except ½ cup cheese. Cover with foil; bake at 350°F for 45 minutes. Uncover; sprinkle evenly with remaining ½ cup cheese. Bake until potato is fork tender, about 30 to 40 minutes. Serve.

Calories 320; **fat calories** 190; **total fat** 21g; **sat fat** 13g; **cholesterol** 60mg; **sodium** 320mg; **total carbohydrates** 19g; **fiber** 2g; **sugars** 6g; **protein** 15g; **vitamin A IUs** 15%; **vitamin C** 80%; **calcium** 40%; **iron** 5%

Heat It Up!
Kick up the heat a notch by adding a Hungarian wax or banana chile pepper to the mix.

De Arbol

DRIED

CHILE-ROASTED DUTCH YELLOW POTATOES 🌶🌶

This easy recipe invites experimentation with different colored potatoes and different chile peppers.

PREP TIME: **15 MIN.** / TOTAL TIME: **45 MIN.** / SERVES: **6 (ABOUT 1 CUP)**

1½ pounds baby Dutch yellow potatoes, halved

2 tablespoons extra-virgin olive oil

4 dried de arbol chile peppers, stems and seeds removed, ground

2 sprigs fresh rosemary, stems removed

1 teaspoon kosher salt

1 teaspoon freshly ground black pepper

1. Preheat oven to 425°F. In a bowl, combine all ingredients; toss together. Arrange in a single layer on a baking sheet; bake at 425°F until fork tender, stirring halfway through, about 15 to 18 minutes. Gently toss together. Garnish with additional rosemary sprigs, if desired. Serve.

Calories 150; **fat calories** 70; **total fat** 8g; **sat fat** 0.5g; **cholesterol** 0mg; **sodium** 675mg; **total carbohydrates** 19g; **fiber** 3g; **sugars** 1g; **protein** 2g; **vitamin A IUs** 4%; **vitamin C** 35%; **calcium** 2%; **iron** 6%

POTATO AND CAULIFLOWER CHEESE BAKE ⁊⁊

Ancho

DRIED

Add a bit of color with a mix of red, purple, and yellow potatoes.

PREP TIME: **40 MIN.** / TOTAL TIME: **1 HR. 25 MIN.** / SERVES: **8 (ABOUT 2 CUPS)**

1½ pounds baby Dutch yellow
   potatoes, halved
1 head cauliflower, cut into
   florets (about 2¼ pounds)
2 tablespoons extra-virgin
   olive oil
Salt
Freshly ground white pepper
3 cups shredded sharp cheddar
   cheese (about 12 ounces)
⅓ cup heavy cream
3 dried ancho chile peppers,
   stems and seeds removed
2 garlic cloves, minced

1. Preheat oven to 425°F. Line a baking dish with foil. In a large saucepan, combine potatoes and enough salted water to cover; bring just to boiling. Reduce heat; simmer until potatoes are just tender, about 10 minutes. Drain.
2. In a bowl, combine cauliflower and oil; toss together. Arrange in a single layer in prepared baking dish. Bake at 425°F until just tender and lightly browned, about 10 to 15 minutes.
3. Butter bottom and sides of a 13 x 9–inch baking dish. Place potatoes and cauliflower in baking dish; sprinkle with salt and white pepper to taste. Top evenly with cheese and cream. Bake at 425°F until heated through and cheese

is melted, about 15 minutes.
4. In a medium saucepan, combine chile and enough water to cover; bring just to boiling. Reduce heat; simmer 5 minutes. Remove from heat; drain over a bowl, reserving chile water. Place chile, garlic, and ¼ cup reserved chile water in a blender*; process until smooth, adding more chile water as needed to reach desired thickness. Stir in salt to taste. Drizzle chile mixture over vegetables. Serve.

Note: *Be cautious when blending hot foods; the contents expand rapidly, causing a risk of scalding. To be safe, before blending, remove center piece of blender lid (to allow steam to escape), secure lid on blender, and place a towel over opening in lid (to avoid splatters).*

Calories 450; **fat calories** 220; **total fat** 24g; **sat fat** 12g; **cholesterol** 60mg; **sodium** 780mg; **total carbohydrates** 46g; **fiber** 5g; **sugars** 3g; **protein** 15g; **vitamin A IUs** 70%; **vitamin C** 120%; **calcium** 35%; **iron** 8%

MALT VINEGAR SMASHED POTATOES ,,

The tang of the malt vinegar spikes the heat of the chiles while dissipating the burn.

DRIED

PREP TIME: **20 MIN.** / TOTAL TIME: **1 HR.** / SERVES: **6 (4 SMASHED POTATOES)**

24 baby Dutch yellow potatoes (about 2 pounds)
Canola oil for frying (about ½ cup)
Malt vinegar
Garlic salt
20 dried pequin chile peppers, finely ground (about 1 teaspoon)

1. In a large saucepan, combine potatoes and enough salted water to cover; bring just to boiling. Cook until fork tender, about 20 to 25 minutes. Drain; pat potatoes dry with paper towels.
2. Gently smash each potato to about ½-inch thickness. Heat about ½ inch oil in a large straight-sided sauté pan to 365°F. Fry potatoes in batches, without over-crowding sauté pan, until crispy and golden brown, about 5 minutes per side. Transfer to paper towels to drain.
3. Drizzle potatoes evenly with malt vinegar to taste; sprinkle with garlic salt and chile to taste. Serve.

Calories 310; **fat calories** 210; **total fat** 23g; **sat fat** 1.5g; **cholesterol** 0mg; **sodium** 1,230mg; **total carbohydrates** 27g; **fiber** 5g; **sugars** 2g; **protein** 3g; **vitamin A IUs** 6%; **vitamin C** 60%; **calcium** 4%; **iron** 6%

Kitchen Savvy
Use a large, flat spatula to gently smash each potato.

Jalapeño

FRESH

GLAZED CHILE-SPICED BABY CARROTS 〃

Mix it up a bit by using half carrots and half parsnips.

PREP TIME: **10 MIN.** / TOTAL TIME: **25 MIN.** / SERVES: **4 (ABOUT 1 CUP)**

Simple Swap

Instead of baby carrots, you can also use regular carrots cut into thick rounds.

3 tablespoons unsalted butter
2 tablespoons extra-virgin olive oil
2 large fresh jalapeño chile peppers, stems and seeds removed, finely diced
¼ cup packed brown sugar
1 pound thin carrots, ends trimmed
Salt

1. Heat butter and oil in a large skillet over medium-high heat. Add chile, brown sugar, and carrots; cook until carrots are slightly softened, stirring occasionally, about 10 minutes. Stir in salt to taste. Serve.

Calories 250; **fat calories** 130; **total fat** 15g; **sat fat** 6g; **cholesterol** 25mg; **sodium** 65mg; **total carbohydrates** 27g; **fiber** 3g; **sugars** 21g; **protein** 2g; **vitamin A IUs** 340%; **vitamin C** 60%; **calcium** 4%; **iron** 2%

Chilaca

FRESH

Bell Pepper

FRESH

ASPARAGUS, ARTICHOKE, AND CHILACA SAUTÉ ⸝

This summery sauté can also top grilled chicken or steak.

PREP TIME: **25 MIN.** / TOTAL TIME: **50 MIN.** / SERVES: **6 (ABOUT 1 CUP)**

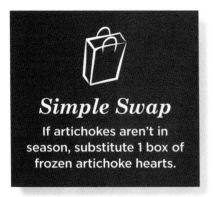

Simple Swap

If artichokes aren't in season, substitute 1 box of frozen artichoke hearts.

12 baby artichokes
1 tablespoon lemon juice
¾ pound asparagus, trimmed
2 tablespoons extra-virgin olive oil
3 fresh chilaca chile peppers, charred, peeled, stems and seeds removed, and sliced into strips
1 large fresh red bell pepper, stem and seeds removed, sliced into strips
2 garlic cloves, minced
Salt
Freshly ground black pepper

1. Snap off outer layer of petals from artichokes until you reach pale, yellow-green layer of petals. With a sharp knife, trim stem ends and remove the rest of the dark green outer part of the stem. Cut about half an inch off the top of each artichoke. Slice artichokes in half; transfer to a bowl of cold water mixed with lemon juice.
2. Bring a large saucepan of salted water just to boiling. Drain artichokes. Add artichokes and asparagus to saucepan; return to boiling. Reduce heat; simmer 2 minutes. Remove asparagus; plunge into ice water. Simmer artichokes until tender, about 4 to 5 minutes; plunge into ice water. Drain asparagus and artichokes; transfer to paper towels to dry.
3. Heat oil in a large skillet over medium-high heat. Add artichokes, asparagus, chile, bell pepper, and garlic; cook until lightly browned, about 5 minutes. Sprinkle with salt and black pepper to taste. Serve.

Calories 100; **fat calories** 45; **total fat** 5g; **sat fat** 0.5g; **cholesterol** 0mg; **sodium** 450mg; **total carbohydrates** 11g; **fiber** 6g; **sugars** 3g; **protein** 3g; **vitamin A IUs** 30%; **vitamin C** 90%; **calcium** 6%; **iron** 10%

BABY ARTICHOKES WITH CHILE-CREAM SAUCE 🌶🌶🌶

Bhut Jolokia

DRIED

Serve this creamy Sicilian-style dish with grilled bread.

PREP TIME: **20 MIN.** / TOTAL TIME: **45 MIN.** / SERVES: **6 (ABOUT 1½ CUPS)**

- 12 baby artichokes
- 4 tablespoons lemon juice, divided (about 1 large lemon)
- ¼ cup extra-virgin olive oil
- 1 large sweet onion, diced (about 1 cup)
- 5 garlic cloves, 4 halved and 1 minced
- 1 cup cherry tomatoes (about ½ pint), halved
- 1 lime, juiced (about 2 tablespoons juice)

Salt

Freshly ground black pepper

- 1 cup mayonnaise
- 1 cup heavy cream
- 1 dried bhut jolokia chile pepper, stem and seeds removed, halved

1. Snap off outer layer of petals from artichokes until you reach pale, yellow-green layer of petals. With a sharp knife, trim stem ends and remove the rest of the dark green outer part of the stem. Cut about half an inch off the top of each artichoke. Slice artichokes into quarters; transfer to a bowl of cold water mixed with 1 tablespoon lemon juice.

2. Heat oil in a large skillet over medium-high heat. Drain artichokes. Add artichokes, onion, and halved garlic to skillet; cook, stirring occasionally, 5 minutes. Stir in tomato, remaining 3 tablespoons lemon juice, and lime juice. Cook until tomato is softened, about 5 minutes. Stir in salt and black pepper to taste.

3. In a small saucepan, combine mayonnaise, heavy cream, chile, and minced garlic; bring just to boiling. Reduce heat; simmer until slightly thickened, about 5 minutes. Remove chile. Pour sauce over artichoke mixture. Serve.

Calories 520; **fat calories** 470; **total fat** 52g; **sat fat** 15g; **cholesterol** 70mg; **sodium** 300mg; **total carbohydrates** 13g; **fiber** 5g; **sugars** 3g; **protein** 4g; **vitamin A IUs** 20%; **vitamin C** 30%; **calcium** 8%; **iron** 4%

Cool It Down!

Dried bhut jolokia chile peppers are near the top of the Scoville heat scale. Turn down the heat by using dried pequin chile peppers instead.

SWEET-SPICY ROSEMARY VEGGIE KABOBS 𝄇𝄇𝄇

FRESH — Bell Pepper

DRIED — Bhut Jolokia

The rosemary skewers make for a fun presentation and add floral flavor.

PREP TIME: **15 MIN.** / TOTAL TIME: **30 MIN.** / SERVES: **4 (1 SKEWER)**

4	large rosemary sprigs
8	button mushrooms
8	cherry tomatoes
½	eggplant, cut into 8 pieces
½	fresh red bell pepper, stem and seeds removed, cut into 8 pieces
½	fresh yellow bell pepper, stem and seeds removed, cut into 8 pieces
½	fresh green bell pepper, stem and seeds removed, cut into 8 pieces
2	tablespoons sugar
1	dried bhut jolokia chile pepper, stem and seeds removed, ground
Salt	

1. Preheat grill to medium-high heat. Remove leaves from all but the tip of rosemary sprigs. Thread 2 pieces each of mushrooms, tomatoes, eggplant, and each color of bell peppers alternately onto a rosemary skewer. Repeat procedure with remaining skewers and mushrooms, tomatoes, eggplant, and bell peppers. Sprinkle evenly with sugar, chile, and salt. **2.** Place skewers on grill rack; grill until well marked and crisptender, turning several times, about 10 to 12 minutes. Serve.

Calories 80; **fat calories** 5; **total fat** 0g; **sat fat** 0g; **cholesterol** 0mg; **sodium** 10mg; **total carbohydrates** 17g; **fiber** 3g; **sugars** 5g; **protein** 2g; **vitamin A IUs** 45%; **vitamin C** 70%; **calcium** 2%; **iron** 4%

Kitchen Savvy

Soak the rosemary skewers in water for 30 minutes before threading on the vegetables—this keeps them from catching fire on the hot grill.

CHILE-ROASTED POTATOES AND VEGGIES ,,

Pequin

DRIED

Veggie Sweet Mini

FRESH

This recipe also works well with other root vegetables, like carrots and parsnips. Try combining your favorites!

PREP TIME: **20 MIN.** / TOTAL TIME: **40 MIN.** / SERVES: **6 (ABOUT 2 CUPS)**

1½   pounds baby Dutch yellow potatoes, quartered

½   pound fresh green beans, trimmed

15   dried pequin chile peppers, ground (about 1 teaspoon)

1   5-ounce package fresh veggie sweet mini peppers, stems and seeds removed, sliced into thick rounds

3   tablespoons extra-virgin olive oil

Salt

Freshly ground black pepper

3   garlic cloves, minced

1. Preheat oven to 425°F. In a bowl, combine all ingredients except garlic; toss together. Arrange in an even layer in a large roasting pan. Bake at 425°F until potatoes are fork tender, stirring in garlic halfway through, about 18 to 20 minutes. Serve.

Calories 230; **fat calories** 100; **total fat** 12g; **sat fat** 1.5g; **cholesterol** 0mg; **sodium** 770mg; **total carbohydrates** 29g; **fiber** 4g; **sugars** 4g; **protein** 4g; **vitamin A IUs** 20%; **vitamin C** 60%; **calcium** 4%; **iron** 8%

Chilaca

FRESH

GRILLED SWEET CORN WITH CHILACA CHILE BUTTER 〟

Create your own flavorful butter combination, called compound butter, and serve with grilled steaks and seafood.

PREP TIME: **10 MIN.** / TOTAL TIME: **2 HR. 10 MIN.** / SERVES: **6 (1 EAR OF CORN)**

Make Ahead

The chilaca butter can be refrigerated, tightly sealed, for up to one week.

8 tablespoons unsalted butter, softened
3 fresh chilaca chile peppers, charred, peeled, stems and seeds removed, finely diced
1 garlic clove, minced
Salt
Freshly ground black pepper
6 ears sweet corn, husked and cleaned

1. In a bowl, combine butter, chile, and garlic; stir in salt and black pepper to taste. Cover with a sheet of plastic wrap. Refrigerate until firm, 2 hours or overnight.
2. Preheat grill to medium-high heat. Place corn on grill rack; grill until golden brown and slightly charred on all sides, about 10 minutes. Top evenly with chile butter. Serve.

Calories 260; **fat calories** 120; **total fat** 13g; **sat fat** 7g; **cholesterol** 30mg; **sodium** 430mg; **total carbohydrates** 37g; **fiber** 5g; **sugars** 13g; **protein** 6g; **vitamin A IUs** 8%; **vitamin C** 20%; **calcium** 0%; **iron** 6%

ROASTED POBLANO MAC 'N' CHEESE ⟩⟩

Poblano

FRESH

If you don't have foil loaf pans, use other small baking dishes.

PREP TIME: **25 MIN.** / TOTAL TIME: **1 HR. 15 MIN.** / SERVES: **12 (1½ CUPS)**

1   16-ounce box cavatappi or macaroni pasta
3   tablespoons olive oil, divided
8   tablespoons unsalted butter (½ cup)
½   cup all-purpose flour
2   cups milk
1   cup crema or crème fraîche
½   teaspoon freshly grated nutmeg
2   cups preshredded cheddar-Jack cheese (about 8 ounces)
2   cups preshredded Gouda cheese (about 8 ounces)
1½ teaspoons smoked paprika, divided
Salt
Freshly ground white pepper
4   fresh poblano chile peppers, charred, peeled, stems and seeds removed, finely diced
¾   cup panko (Japanese breadcrumbs)

1. Prepare pasta according to package directions; drain. Drizzle with about 1 tablespoon oil to keep pasta from sticking.
2. Preheat oven to 350°F. Coat insides of 6 (6 x 2–inch) foil loaf pans with cooking spray. Melt butter in a large saucepan over medium heat; whisk in flour until a smooth paste is formed, about 3 minutes. Whisk in milk, crema, and nutmeg until smooth; whisk in cheeses until completely melted. Whisk in 1 teaspoon paprika; whisk in salt and white pepper to taste. Remove from heat.
3. Add pasta and poblano chile to cheese mixture; toss together. Pour evenly into prepared pans. In a bowl, combine remaining 2 tablespoons oil, remaining ½ teaspoon paprika, and breadcrumbs; stir in salt to taste. Sprinkle evenly over pasta mixture. Bake at 350°F until bubbly and lightly browned, about 25 minutes. Let rest 5 minutes. Serve.

Calories 520; **fat calories** 267; **total fat** 30g; **sat fat** 18g; **cholesterol** 90mg; **sodium** 300mg; **total carbohydrates** 45g; **fiber** 2g; **sugars** 8g; **protein** 18g; **vitamin A IUs** 33%; **vitamin C** 207%; **calcium** 23%; **iron** 10%

Heat It Up!
Add a touch more heat to this chile mac by substituting a large hot banana chile pepper for one of the poblano chile peppers.

Poblano

FRESH

SHREDDED BRUSSELS SPROUT SLAW ⟩⟩

Stir in some zest from the lemon for a little extra pizzazz.

PREP TIME: **20 MIN.** / TOTAL TIME: **2 HR. 25 MIN.** / SERVES: **8 (ABOUT 1½ CUPS)**

Heat It Up!
Try fresh Cubanelle chile peppers instead of the poblano to kick up the heat.

2   pounds Brussels sprouts, trimmed and shredded
2   carrots, shredded (1 cup)
2   fresh poblano chile peppers, roasted, peeled, stems and seeds removed, finely diced
2   garlic cloves, minced
1   leek, trimmed and thinly sliced (about ½ cup)
¾   cup plain Greek yogurt
⅓   cup sugar
¼   cup whole milk
4   teaspoons seasoned rice vinegar
1   tablespoon white wine vinegar
1   lemon, juiced (about 3 tablespoons juice)
Salt
Freshly ground black pepper

1. In a large bowl, combine Brussels sprouts and next 4 ingredients (through leek).
2. Place yogurt and next 5 ingredients (through juice) in a blender; process on low speed until smooth. Stir in salt and black pepper to taste.
3. Add yogurt mixture to Brussels sprouts mixture; toss together. Cover and refrigerate at least 2 hours. Serve.

Calories 180; **fat calories** 30; **total fat** 3.5g; **sat fat** 2g; **cholesterol** 5mg; **sodium** 260mg; **total carbohydrates** 32g; **fiber** 7g; **sugars** 18g; **protein** 6g; **vitamin A IUs** 170%; **vitamin C** 330%; **calcium** 10%; **iron** 8%

COLE SLAW WITH CHILE-LIME DRESSING "

You could also serve this Southeast Asian slaw as a bed for teriyaki grilled beef skewers or steamed fish.

PREP TIME: **20 MIN.** / TOTAL TIME: **2 HR. 25 MIN.** / SERVES: **8 (ABOUT 2 CUPS)**

Serrano

FRESH

- 1 pound Brussels sprouts, trimmed and shredded
- 1 pound napa cabbage, shredded
- ¾ pound red cabbage, shredded
- 2 carrots, shredded (about 1 cup)
- ½ cup mayonnaise
- ⅓ cup sugar
- ¼ cup whole milk
- ¼ cup buttermilk
- 4 teaspoons seasoned rice vinegar
- 1 tablespoon white wine vinegar
- ¼ teaspoon salt
- 2 garlic cloves, minced
- 2 limes, juiced (about ¼ cup juice)
- 1 fresh serrano chile pepper, stem removed, finely chopped

1. In a large bowl, combine Brussels sprouts, cabbages, and carrot. In a bowl, whisk together remaining ingredients until smooth. Add to cabbage mixture; toss together. Cover and refrigerate at least 2 hours. Serve.

Calories 130; **fat calories** 25; **total fat** 2.5g; **sat fat** 0g; **cholesterol** 0mg; **sodium** 590mg; **total carbohydrates** 24g; **fiber** 5g; **sugars** 15g; **protein** 4g; **vitamin A IUs** 150%; **vitamin C** 150%; **calcium** 8%; **iron** 4%

Make Ahead

Let the flavors develop even more by making this spicy slaw the day before.

DRIED

De Arbol

Simple Swap

If broccolini is unavailable, substitute bagged broccoli florets.

BROCCOLINI-CHILE SAUTÉ 🌶🌶

Broccolini is similar to broccoli but with thinner stalks and smaller florets.

PREP TIME: **15 MIN.** / TOTAL TIME: **30 MIN.** / SERVES: **4 (ABOUT 1½ CUPS)**

3　dried de arbol chile peppers, stems and seeds removed, divided
1　pound broccolini, trimmed and cut into bite-size pieces
2　tablespoons extra-virgin olive oil
2　garlic cloves, minced
1　tomato, diced (about ⅔ cup)
1　large lemon, juiced (about ¼ cup juice)
Salt
Freshly ground black pepper
Fresh lemon, thinly sliced (optional)

1. Fill a large large saucepan three-fourths full with salted water. Add 1 chile; bring just to boiling. Add broccolini. Cover; cook until slightly tender, about 5 minutes. Drain; rinse with cold water. Drain.
2. Heat oil in a large skillet over medium-high heat. Add remaining 2 chiles; cook 1 minute. Add broccolini, garlic, and tomato; cook 3 minutes. Add juice; cook 2 minutes. Stir in salt, black pepper, and lemon slices, if desired. Serve.

Calories 150; **fat calories** 80; **total fat** 9g; **sat fat** 1.5g; **cholesterol** 0mg; **sodium** 830mg; **total carbohydrates** 14g; **fiber** 1g; **sugars** 4g; **protein** 6g; **vitamin A IUs** 210%; **vitamin C** 270%; **calcium** 8%; **iron** 8%

New Mexico

DRIED

ROASTED SPAGHETTI SQUASH ⸰

Similar to pasta, the thin strands from the squash make an excellent side to any Italian main dish.

PREP TIME: **25 MIN.** / TOTAL TIME: **1 HR. 7 MIN.** / SERVES: **6 (½ SQUASH)**

Kitchen Savvy

For a quicker side, carefully cut spaghetti squash in half, scoop out the seeds, and microwave the halves (flesh facing down) in about 1 inch of water for 5 minutes.

½   pound thick-cut bacon, diced
3   small spaghetti squash, halved and seeded (about 2½ pounds)
2   garlic cloves, minced
2   dried New Mexico chiles, stems and seeds removed, ground
1   sweet onion, thinly sliced (about ¾ cup)
6   tablespoons unsalted butter, cut into 6 pieces
Salt
Freshly ground black pepper

1. Preheat oven to 400°F. Heat a large skillet over medium-high heat. Add bacon; cook until crisp, stirring occasionally, about 7 minutes. Transfer to paper towels to drain. Reserve bacon grease, if desired.
2. Place squash halves on a baking sheet, cut side up. Top squash halves evenly with bacon, garlic, chile, and onion. Cut each tablespoon of butter into 4 pieces; top squash halves evenly with butter. Sprinkle with salt and black pepper. Drizzle evenly with some of reserved bacon grease, if desired. Bake at 400°F until fork tender, about 35 to 45 minutes. Scrape out squash strands; discard shells. Serve.

Calories 400; **fat calories** 280; **total fat** 31g; **sat fat** 15g; **cholesterol** 80mg; **sodium** 1,020mg; **total carbohydrates** 22g; **fiber** 3g; **sugars** 8g; **protein** 12g; **vitamin A IUs** 25%; **vitamin C** 15%; **calcium** 4%; **iron** 4%

ROASTED ANAHEIM NAVY BEANS

Sometimes small rocks can sneak into dried beans—make sure you rinse and clean the beans thoroughly.

Bell Pepper
FRESH

Anaheim
FRESH

PREP TIME: **30 MIN.** / TOTAL TIME: **2 HR. 50 MIN.** / SERVES: **12 (ABOUT 1¾ CUPS)**

2   smoked ham hocks (about 2 pounds)
1   ham hock (about 1 pound)
3   tablespoons extra-virgin olive oil
4   ribs celery, finely chopped (about 1½ cups)
2   large Roma tomatoes, finely chopped (about 1 cup)
2   garlic cloves, minced
1   large sweet onion, finely chopped (about 1½ cups)
1   fresh red bell pepper, stem and seeds removed, finely chopped (about ½ cup)
½   teaspoon dried oregano, crushed
Freshly ground black pepper
12   large fresh Anaheim chile peppers, charred, peeled, stems and seeds removed, diced (about 1¾ pounds)
1   pound dried navy beans, rinsed and cleaned
6   cups chicken broth

1. Score ham hocks with a sharp knife. Heat oil in a large Dutch oven over medium-high heat. Add non-smoked ham hock; brown on all sides. Add celery and next 5 ingredients (through oregano); stir in black pepper. Add smoked ham hocks; cook, stirring often, 3 minutes. Add chile, beans, and broth; bring just to boiling. Reduce heat and cover; simmer until beans are tender, about 2 hours. Place 2 cups bean mixture in a blender*; process until smooth. Return blended bean mixture to Dutch oven. Serve.

***Note:** Be cautious when blending hot foods; the contents expand rapidly, causing a risk of scalding. To be safe, before blending, remove center piece of blender lid (to allow steam to escape), secure lid on blender, and place a towel over opening in lid (to avoid splatters).*

Calories 483; **fat calories** 242; **total fat** 27g; **sat fat** 8g; **cholesterol** 63mg; **sodium** 875mg; **total carbohydrates** 36g; **fiber** 11g; **sugars** 8g; **protein** 27g; **vitamin A IUs** 25%; **vitamin C** 317%; **calcium** 8%; **iron** 21%

Simple Swap

The fresh ham hock adds a ton of meaty flavor, but if you can't find an un-smoked version in your local grocery store, add cooked cubed ham right before serving.

CHIPOTLE-MAPLE BAKED BEANS 〃

The combination of smoke, sweet, and spice makes this chuck wagon classic irresistible. Use only pure maple syrup.

PREP TIME: **20 MIN.** / TOTAL TIME: **4 HR. 40 MIN.** / SERVES: **12 (ABOUT 1 CUP)**

- 1 pound dry pinto beans, rinsed and drained
- 2 tablespoons extra-virgin olive oil
- 1 large sweet onion, finely chopped (about 2 cups)
- ½ pound maple-flavored bacon, finely chopped
- ¾ cup pure maple syrup
- ¼ cup packed brown sugar
- ¼ cup ketchup
- 2 tablespoons tomato paste
- 1 tablespoon chipotle chile pepper, canned in adobo sauce, finely diced
- 1 teaspoon salt
- 1 teaspoon freshly ground black pepper
- 3 dried chipotle chile peppers, stems and seeds removed
- 4 cups water
- 2 vanilla beans or 1 teaspoon pure vanilla extract

1. In a large saucepan, combine beans and enough water to cover by 2 inches, about 6 cups total.
2. Preheat oven to 250°F. Heat oil in a Dutch oven over medium-high heat. Add onion; cook until browned, stirring once, about 10 minutes. Add bacon; cook until crisp, about 10 minutes. Stir in maple syrup and next 7 ingredients (through chile).
3. Drain and rinse beans; add to pan. Add 4 cups water. Split vanilla beans in half lengthwise and scrape out seeds; add seeds and pods (or vanilla extract) to Dutch oven. Bring just to boiling. Cover and bake at 250°F until beans are tender, checking occasionally to make sure they do not dry out (stir in more water, if necessary), about 4 to 4½ hours. Serve.

Calories 333; **fat calories** 100; **total fat** 11g; **sat fat** 3g; **cholesterol** 20mg; **sodium** 513mg; **total carbohydrates** 47g; **fiber** 9g; **sugars** 20g; **protein** 14g; **vitamin A IUs** 20%; **vitamin C** 5%; **calcium** 7%; **iron** 13%

Banana Wax

FRESH

Bell Pepper

FRESH

VEGETABLE QUINOA 🌶🌶

For a colorful twist, try red quinoa instead of the regular kind.

PREP TIME: **20 MIN.** / TOTAL TIME: **42 MIN.** / SERVES: **8 (ABOUT 1½ CUPS)**

1 8-ounce package quinoa
2 tablespoons extra-virgin olive oil
2 sweet onions, finely diced (about 1 cup)
2 fresh banana wax chile peppers, stems and seeds removed, sliced into rounds
1 fresh red bell pepper, stem and seeds removed, diced (about ½ cup)
½ carrot, diced (about ¼ cup)
½ zucchini, diced (about ⅔ cup)
½ yellow squash, diced (about ⅔ cup)
2 garlic cloves, minced
Salt
Freshly ground black pepper

1. Prepare quinoa according to package directions.

2. Heat oil in a large skillet over high heat. Add onion and next 5 ingredients (through squash); cook, stirring occasionally, 5 minutes. Add garlic; cook until fragrant, about 1 minute.

3. In a bowl, combine quinoa and vegetable mixture; stir in salt and black pepper to taste. Serve.

Calories 200; **fat calories** 60; **total fat** 7g; **sat fat** 1g; **cholesterol** 0mg; **sodium** 350mg; **total carbohydrates** 29g; **fiber** 4g; **sugars** 5g; **protein** 6g; **vitamin A IUs** 100%; **vitamin C** 110%; **calcium** 4%; **iron** 15%

Bhut Jolokia

FRESH

BASMATI AND WILD RICE WITH GRILLED CORN 🌶🌶🌶

Use this recipe to put some fire into any of your favorite pilaf mixes.

PREP TIME: **20 MIN.** / TOTAL TIME: **50 MIN.** / SERVES: **8 (ABOUT ¾ CUP)**

Cool It Down!

For less heat, substitute fresh cayenne or habanero chile pepper for the bhut jolokia.

2 ears fresh sweet corn, husked and cleaned
2 tablespoons unsalted butter
1 6-ounce package basmati–wild rice pilaf mix
¼ fresh bhut jolokia chile pepper, stem and seeds removed
2 cups low-sodium chicken broth
Salt

1. Preheat grill to medium-high heat. Place corn on grill rack; grill until slightly charred, about 10 minutes. Cool until can be handled, about 15 minutes. Carefully cut kernels from cobs.
2. Melt butter in a medium saucepan over medium-high heat. Add rice mix (omit any seasoning packets) and chile; cook, stirring constantly, 3 minutes. Add broth; bring just to boiling. Reduce heat and cover; simmer until liquid has been absorbed, about 15 minutes. Remove from heat. Remove and discard chile. Stir in corn and salt to taste. Let sit 5 minutes; fluff with a fork. Serve.

Calories 130; **fat calories** 30; **total fat** 3.5g; **sat fat** 2g; **cholesterol** 10mg; **sodium** 470mg; **total carbohydrates** 24g; **fiber** 2g; **sugars** 2g; **protein** 3g; **vitamin A IUs** 4%; **vitamin C** 2%; **calcium** 0%; **iron** 4%

 Side Dishes

COUSCOUS WITH CHILES AND GRILLED VEGETABLES ›

Bell Pepper

FRESH

Shishito

FRESH

Couscous is very versatile; try using different chile peppers to liven it up.

PREP TIME: **30 MIN.** / TOTAL TIME: **50 MIN.** / SERVES: **8 (ABOUT 1 CUP)**

1 **6-ounce package couscous**
6 **asparagus stalks, trimmed (about ¼ pound)**
1 **large fresh green bell pepper, halved, stem and seeds removed**
1 **large fresh red bell pepper, halved, stem and seeds removed**
1 **large fresh yellow bell pepper, halved, stem and seeds removed**
6 **fresh shishito chile peppers, stems and seeds removed, split lengthwise**
Extra-virgin olive oil
Salt
Freshly ground black pepper

1. Preheat grill to medium-high heat. Prepare couscous according to package directions.
2. Bring a large saucepan of water just to boiling. Add asparagus; cook until bright green, about 1 to 2 minutes. Drain. Rinse with cold water; drain. Transfer to paper towels.
3. Brush asparagus, bell peppers, and chile with oil; sprinkle with salt and black pepper. Place vegetables on grill rack; grill until slightly charred, about 10 minutes. Cool until can be handled; coarsely chop vegetables. Stir into couscous. Serve.

Calories 160; **fat calories** 60; **total fat** 7g; **sat fat** 1g; **cholesterol** 0mg; **sodium** 300mg; **total carbohydrates** 21g; **fiber** 2g; **sugars** 2g; **protein** 4g; **vitamin A IUs** 15%; **vitamin C** 150%; **calcium** 2%; **iron** 4%

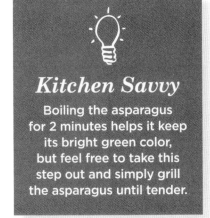

Kitchen Savvy

Boiling the asparagus for 2 minutes helps it keep its bright green color, but feel free to take this step out and simply grill the asparagus until tender.

HABANERO-
TANGERINE
ICE CREAM

desserts

HABANERO-TANGERINE ICE CREAM 🌶🌶🌶

This cool combination of spicy and sweet brings delicious relief on a hot summer day.

PREP TIME: **35 MIN.** / TOTAL TIME: **2 HR.** / SERVES: **12 (ABOUT ½ CUP)**

2 cups whole milk
1 cup heavy cream
2 vanilla beans, split lengthwise
¾ cup sugar, divided
1 fresh habanero chile pepper, stem and seeds removed, finely diced
4 large egg yolks
½ teaspoon pure vanilla extract
4 pounds sweet tangerines, 6 zested, all juiced (about 12)

1. In a large saucepan, combine milk and cream. Scrape vanilla bean seeds into milk mixture; add pods. Stir in ½ cup sugar; bring just to a simmer. Remove from heat. Stir in chile; stir continuously for 2 minutes. Remove vanilla bean pods and discard.

2. In a bowl, combine egg yolks and remaining ¼ cup sugar; whisk vigorously until yolks are pale yellow in color and flow in a steady stream when you lift the whisk. Add about ½ cup milk mixture to egg mixture, stirring constantly. Add egg-milk mixture to milk mixture in saucepan; cook over low heat until thick enough to coat the back of a spoon, stirring often, about 15 minutes. Strain into a bowl; stir in vanilla extract, zest, and juice. Refrigerate until cool.

3. Transfer egg-milk mixture to an ice cream maker; freeze according to manufacturer directions. Serve.

Calories 240; **fat calories** 100; **total fat** 11g; **sat fat** 6g; **cholesterol** 95mg; **sodium** 30mg; **total carbohydrates** 36g; **fiber** 3g; **sugars** 31g; **protein** 4g; **vitamin A IUs** 30%; **vitamin C** 70%; **calcium** 10%; **iron** 2%

HOT AND COLD LEMON-LIME SORBET 〃

Jalapeño
FRESH

Red Fresno
FRESH

For a grown-up twist, stir in a splash of vodka before freezing.

PREP TIME: **25 MIN.** / TOTAL TIME: **1 HR. 32 MIN.** / SERVES: **8 (ABOUT ½ CUP)**

1 cup water
1 cup sugar
1 small or ½ large fresh jalapeño chile pepper, stem and seeds removed, finely diced
½ fresh red Fresno chile pepper, stem and seeds removed, finely diced
2 lemons, 1 zested, both juiced (about ⅓ cup juice)
2 limes, 1 zested, both juiced (about ¼ cup juice)

1. In a medium saucepan, combine 1 cup water, sugar, and chiles; bring just to boiling, stirring constantly. Remove from heat; stir in zests and juices. Refrigerate until completely cooled.
2. Transfer chile mixture to an ice cream maker; freeze according to manufacturer directions. Serve.

Calories 110; **fat calories** 0; **total fat** 0g; **sat fat** 0g; **cholesterol** 0mg; **sodium** 0mg; **total carbohydrates** 28g; **fiber** 0g; **sugars** 26g; **protein** 0g; **vitamin A IUs** 2%; **vitamin C** 30%; **calcium** 0%; **iron** 0%

Make Ahead
Make this summer delight up to a week ahead and store in an airtight container in the freezer.

RASPBERRY ICE CREAM SUNDAES ⟩

For a holiday treat, try making the bark with white chocolate and pistachios instead of dark chocolate and pepitas.

California

DRIED

PREP TIME: **40 MIN.** / TOTAL TIME: **1 HR. 27 MIN.** / SERVES: **6 (1 SUNDAE)**

4   ounces dark chocolate, chopped
⅓   cup pepitas (hulled pumpkin seeds), toasted, divided
3   tablespoons finely ground dried California chile peppers, divided
1   tablespoon orange zest, divided
¼   teaspoon smoked paprika
1½ cups fresh raspberries
2   tablespoons orange juice
⅛   teaspoon salt
1   quart purchased vanilla bean ice cream

1. Line a baking sheet with parchment paper. In a glass bowl, heat chocolate in the microwave on medium until completely melted, stirring with a wooden spoon at 30-second intervals, about 2 minutes. Immediately stir in half of pepitas, 2 teaspoons ground chile, ½ tablespoon orange zest, and paprika.

2. Spoon chocolate mixture onto prepared baking sheet, spreading to an even thickness. Sprinkle with remaining half of pepitas, half of remaining ground chile, and remaining ½ tablespoon orange zest. Refrigerate until hardened, about 45 minutes. Break into 6 pieces.

3. Place remaining chile powder, raspberries, juice, and salt in a blender; process until smooth.

4. Pour raspberry mixture evenly over ice cream; top evenly with bark. Serve.

Calories 580; **fat calories** 320; **total fat** 36g; **sat fat** 21g; **cholesterol** 140mg; **sodium** 115mg; **total carbohydrates** 56g; **fiber** 3g; **sugars** 40g; **protein** 10g; **vitamin A IUs** 30%; **vitamin C** 15%; **calcium** 15%; **iron** 25%

RASPBERRY-CHILE CRÈME BRÛLÉE)))

Habanero

FRESH

Crème brûlée literally means "broiled cream."

PREP TIME: **20 MIN.** / TOTAL TIME: **5 HR. 30 MIN.** / SERVES: **6 (1 CUSTARD)**

5   large egg yolks
½   cup granulated sugar
1¾ cups heavy cream
1   vanilla bean, split
1   fresh orange habanero chile
    pepper, stem and seeds
    removed, finely diced
1   pint fresh raspberries
Turbinado sugar or superfine sugar
    for sprinkling (about
    3 tablespoons)

1. Preheat oven to 325°F. In a bowl, combine egg yolks and ½ cup granulated sugar; whisk vigorously until yolks are pale yellow in color and flow in a steady stream when you lift the whisk.
2. Pour cream into a small saucepan. Scrape vanilla bean seeds into cream; add pods and chile. Heat just to a simmer over medium-high heat, about 5 minutes. Slowly whisk cream mixture into egg yolk mixture in a thin stream (do not add more than a little at a time or egg yolks will scramble). Strain into a large glass measuring cup.
3. Arrange raspberries evenly in bottoms of 6 (4-ounce) ramekins; top evenly with cream-egg mixture. Arrange ramekins in a shallow roasting pan; pour enough hot water into roasting pan to reach halfway up the outsides of the ramekins. Cover loosely with foil; bake at 325°F until set, about 1 to 1¼ hours. Transfer ramekins to wire racks to cool. Refrigerate 4 hours.
4. Preheat broiler to high. Top each custard with turbinado sugar; broil until golden brown, about 2 minutes. Serve.

Calories 370; **fat calories** 270; **total fat** 30g; **sat fat** 17g; **cholesterol** 250mg; **sodium** 35mg; **total carbohydrates** 26g; **fiber** 0g; **sugars** 17g; **protein** 4g; **vitamin A IUs** 25%; **vitamin C** 15%; **calcium** 8%; **iron** 4%

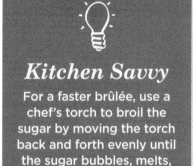

Kitchen Savvy

For a faster brûlée, use a chef's torch to broil the sugar by moving the torch back and forth evenly until the sugar bubbles, melts, and just chars in spots.

BRÛLÉED BANANAS WITH PINEAPPLE SALSA 🌶🌶

Bell Pepper

FRESH

Thai

FRESH

If baby pineapples are unavailable, use a full-size pineapple.

PREP TIME: **25 MIN.** / TOTAL TIME: **35 MIN.** / SERVES: **6 (½ BANANA & 1 CUP SALSA)**

3 bananas, peeled and halved lengthwise

¼ cup packed brown sugar

6 tangerines, 3 segmented, 3 juiced (about 1¾ pounds)

½ fresh green bell pepper, stem and seeds removed, finely diced (about ½ cup)

½ fresh red bell pepper, stem and seeds removed, finely diced (about ½ cup)

½ fresh yellow bell pepper, stem and seeds removed, finely diced (about ½ cup)

1 12-ounce baby pineapple, finely diced (about 1½ cups)

3 fresh Thai chile peppers, stems and seeds removed, finely diced

1. Preheat broiler. Line a baking sheet with foil. Arrange banana halves, cut side up, on prepared baking sheet; sprinkle evenly with brown sugar. Broil until sugar is evenly melted and charred in spots, about 5 to 10 minutes (be careful not to burn).

2. In a large bowl, gently combine tangerine segments, juice, and remaining ingredients. Top bananas evenly with tangerine mixture. Serve.

Calories 150; **fat calories** 5; **total fat** 0.5g; **sat fat** 0g; **cholesterol** 0mg; **sodium** 5mg; **total carbohydrates** 38g; **fiber** 4g; **sugars** 27g; **protein** 2g; **vitamin A IUs** 20%; **vitamin C** 140%; **calcium** 6%; **iron** 4%

Cool It Down!

Tone down the burn by using jalapeño chile peppers in place of the Thai chiles.

Yellow

FRESH

Simple Swap

Purchase refrigerated pie crusts if you don't have time to make homemade dough.

CHOCOLATE, BANANA, AND CHERRY EMPANADAS ⟩⟩

These are the perfect companions to Mexican hot chocolate or sweet café con leche.

PREP TIME: **15 MIN.** / TOTAL TIME: **1 HR.** / SERVES: **30 (1 EMPANADA)**

2 cups all-purpose flour
½ teaspoon salt
16 tablespoons unsalted butter, chilled (1 cup)
½ cup whole milk
4 bananas (about 1½ pounds), chopped
2 tablespoons granulated sugar
½ cup semi-sweet chocolate chips
3 fresh yellow chile peppers, stems and seeds removed, finely diced
1 3-ounce package dried tart cherries
¼ cup heavy cream
2 tablespoons brown sugar

1. Preheat oven to 375°F. Line a baking sheet with parchment paper. In a large bowl, combine flour and salt. Cut in butter with a pastry blender or 2 knives until mixture is crumbly. Add milk; stir with a fork until flour mixture forms a ball. Turn dough out onto a floured work surface; roll out to ⅛ inch thick. Using a 4-inch cookie cutter or drinking glass, cut into 30 rounds.

2. In a medium bowl, combine bananas and granulated sugar; mash together slightly. Stir in chocolate chips, chile, and cherries.

3. Spoon banana mixture evenly onto dough rounds; fold rounds in half. Seal filled pastries with tines of a fork dipped in cold water; arrange on prepared baking sheet. In a bowl, combine cream and brown sugar; brush evenly over pastries. Bake at 375°F until golden brown, about 25 minutes. Serve hot or at room temperature.

Calories 150; **fat calories** 70; **total fat** 8g; **sat fat** 5g; **cholesterol** 20mg; **sodium** 160mg; **total carbohydrates** 18g; **fiber** 1g; **sugars** 9g; **protein** 2g; **vitamin A IUs** 8%; **vitamin C** 25%; **calcium** 2%; **iron** 4%

CHILE-LIME CREAM PUFFS 〃

Serrano

FRESH

Also knows as profiteroles, these light, airy custard-filled pastries can be dusted with powdered sugar or drizzled with chocolate sauce.

PREP TIME: **20 MIN.** / TOTAL TIME: **1 HR. 52 MIN.** / SERVES: **24 (1 CREAM PUFF)**

1	cup all-purpose flour
1	teaspoon sugar
⅛	teaspoon salt
¾	cup water
6	tablespoons unsalted butter
4	large eggs
4	fresh serrano chile peppers, stems and seeds removed, finely chopped, divided
1	cup heavy whipping cream
½	cup whole milk
1	3.5-ounce package instant vanilla pudding mix

1. Preheat oven to 450°F. Line a baking sheet with parchment paper. In a bowl, sift together flour, sugar, and salt.

2. In a large saucepan, combine ³/₄ cup water and butter; bring just to boiling. Remove from heat. Add flour mixture; using a wooden spoon, stir until flour-butter mixture forms a ball and pulls away from the side of the saucepan, about 1 to 2 minutes. Transfer dough to a mixer fitted with a dough paddle; mix dough on low speed to release steam, about 2 to 3 minutes. With mixer on low speed, add eggs, one at a time, allowing each to fully combine with dough before adding the next. Mix in half of chile on low speed.

3. Spoon dough into a pastry bag fitted with a ¹/₂-inch tip; pipe 24 (2-inch) mounds onto prepared baking sheet, about 2 inches apart. Bake at 450°F until golden, about 10 to 15 minutes. Reduce temperature to 350°F; bake at 350°F for 10 minutes. Turn off oven; let puffs rest in oven 10 minutes. Transfer to a wire rack; cool completely.

4. In the bowl of a mixer fitted with a whisk attachment, combine remaining half of chile, cream, milk, and pudding mix; mix on medium speed until soft peaks form, about 1 minute. Cover; refrigerate until completely chilled, about 1 hour.

5. Cut cream puffs in half. Spoon pudding mixture evenly on bottom halves; top with top halves. Serve.

Calories 110; **fat calories** 70; **total fat** 8g; **sat fat** 4.5g; **cholesterol** 55mg; **sodium** 85mg; **total carbohydrates** 9g; **fiber** 0g; **sugars** 4g; **protein** 2g; **vitamin A IUs** 6%; **vitamin C** 0%; **calcium** 2%; **iron** 2%

Heat It Up!

Looking to really warm up this dessert? Try fresh Thai chile peppers instead of the serrano chiles.

Yellow

FRESH

Kitchen Savvy

Spray scissors with cooking spray and use to separate dough strips when adding to the hot oil.

CHURROS FUEGOS ⟩⟩

Churros are essentially long, star-shaped fried donuts.

PREP TIME: **15 MIN.** / TOTAL TIME: **1 HR.** / SERVES: **20 (1 CHURRO)**

1 cup water
2 fresh yellow chile peppers, stems and seeds removed, finely chopped
2½ tablespoons plus ½ cup sugar
1¼ cups canola oil, divided
⅛ teaspoon salt
1 cup all-purpose flour
8 tablespoons unsalted butter, melted (½ cup)
1 teaspoon ground cinnamon

1. In a medium saucepan, combine 1 cup water, chile, 2½ tablespoons granulated sugar, 2 tablespoons oil, and salt; bring just to boiling, stirring often until sugar is completely dissolved. Remove from heat. Add flour; using a wooden spoon, slowly stir until flour-water mixture forms a ball and pulls away from the side of the saucepan, about 1 to 2 minutes.
2. In a large, straight-sided sauté pan, heat remaining oil to 350°F. Spoon dough into a piping bag fitted with a ¹/₂-inch star tip or a zip-top plastic bag with a corner snipped off; pipe 5-inch strips of dough into oil, in batches, to create 20 strips. Cook until golden brown, turning frequently, about 2 to 3 minutes. Carefully remove from oil; transfer to a wire rack over paper towels to drain.
3. In a bowl, combine remaining ¹/₂ cup sugar, butter, and cinnamon; brush over churros. Serve.

Calories 170; **fat calories** 130; **total fat** 14g; **sat fat** 3.5g; **cholesterol** 10mg; **sodium** 15mg; **total carbohydrates** 11g; **fiber** 0g; **sugars** 7g; **protein** 1g; **vitamin A IUs** 4%; **vitamin C** 10%; **calcium** 0%; **iron** 2%

MANGO-FILLED CHILE DONUTS ›

Mulato

DRIED

These fried pillows of sweet dough have fruit-filled centers.

PREP TIME: **30 MIN.** / TOTAL TIME: **2 HR. 15 MIN.** / SERVES: **16 (1 DONUT)**

1 16-ounce loaf frozen bread
   dough, thawed
2 fresh mangos, peeled and
   sliced
1 teaspoon fresh lime juice
½ teaspoon salt
½ cup sugar
1 tablespoon ground cinnamon
1 dried mulato chile pepper,
   stem and seeds removed,
   ground (about 1 tablespoon)
⅔ cup canola oil

1. Line a baking sheet with parchment paper. Divide bread dough into 16 (1-ounce) balls; arrange on prepared baking sheet, about 1 inch apart. Cover with plastic wrap; let rise at least 1 hour.

2. Place mango, juice, and salt in a blender; process until smooth. Transfer to a squeeze bottle or a piping bag fitted with a pastry tip. In a bowl, combine sugar, cinnamon, and chile.

3. Heat oil in a Dutch oven to 325°F. Carefully drop 2 or 3 dough balls at a time into oil. Cook until golden, using metal tongs to turn once, about 3 minutes per side. Using a slotted spoon, transfer to a paper towel–lined plate; sprinkle with sugar mixture. Repeat procedure with remaining dough balls. Let stand until cool.

4. Carefully poke a hole into side of each donut with squeeze bottle or pastry tip and fill with mango mixture. Serve.

Calories 210; **fat calories** 90; **total fat** 11g; **sat fat** 0.5g; **cholesterol** 0mg; **sodium** 230mg; **total carbohydrates** 27g; **fiber** 1g; **sugars** 12g; **protein** 3g; **vitamin A IUs** 10%; **vitamin C** 25%; **calcium** 0%; **iron** 6%

BUÑUELOS WITH HOT HONEY DRIZZLE 〟〟〟

Bhut Jolokia

DRIED

Jazz up these sweet, crispy tortilla chips with a sprinkle of ground cinnamon and sugar.

PREP TIME: **5 MIN.** / TOTAL TIME: **25 MIN.** / SERVES: **6 (1 TORTILLA)**

½ cup honey
1 dried bhut jolokia (ghost) chile pepper, split lengthwise, stem and seeds removed
Canola oil
6 (8-inch) flour tortillas

1. In a small saucepan, combine honey and chile. Bring to a simmer; remove from heat. Let sit 15 minutes; remove and discard chile.

2. In a large, straight-sided sauté pan, heat about 1 inch of oil to 375°F. Fry tortillas one at a time until golden, about 15 seconds per side. Transfer to paper towels to drain. Drizzle with honey mixture. Serve.

Calories 410; **fat calories** 200; **total fat** 22g; **sat fat** 3g; **cholesterol** 0mg; **sodium** 440mg; **total carbohydrates** 49g; **fiber** 1g; **sugars** 22g; **protein** 4g; **vitamin A IUs** 2%; **vitamin C** 0%; **calcium** 0%; **iron** % 0

Cool It Down!

Dried mulato chile pepper is much tamer than the infamous bhut jolokia chile pepper; use it in place of the bhut jolokia to make this a kid-friendly treat.

Ancho

DRIED

Cayenne

FRESH

THE DEVIL'S FAVORITE DEVIL'S FOOD CAKE ❞

Ancho chile pepper has a hint of cocoa flavor, making it an excellent partner for chocolate.

PREP TIME: **20 MIN.** / TOTAL TIME: **3 HR.** / SERVES: **16 (1 PIECE)**

Cake

2	cups sugar
1¾	cups all-purpose flour
¾	cup cocoa powder
2	teaspoons ground ancho chile powder
1	teaspoon salt
1	cup whole milk
½	cup grapeseed or canola oil
2	tablespoons espresso syrup or coffee extract or 2 teaspoons espresso coffee powder
2	large eggs
¾	cup water

Ganache

½	cup heavy cream
1	fresh cayenne chile pepper, stem and seeds removed
12	ounces semi-sweet chocolate chips
1	teaspoon salted butter

1. To make cake, preheat oven to 350°F. Spray a 13 x 9 x 2–inch baking pan with cooking spray; dust with flour. In a bowl, sift together sugar and next 4 ingredients (through salt); add milk, oil, espresso, and eggs. Using an electric mixer, mix on low speed 1 minute, then on medium speed 2 minutes.
2. In a small saucepan, bring ³⁄₄ cup water to a boil. Drizzle boiling water into batter, stirring until blended. Pour batter into prepared baking pan. Bake at 350°F until a toothpick inserted in center comes out clean, about 40 minutes. Cool completely.
3. To make ganache, in a small saucepan, bring cream just to a simmer. Remove from heat; stir in cayenne chile. Let sit at least 30 minutes; discard chile. Reheat cream to a simmer. Remove cream from heat; immediately add chocolate chips, stirring until just melted. Add butter; whisk until glossy and smooth. Let sit 30 minutes.
4. Pour ganache evenly over cake (make sure top is completely covered). Chill in the refrigerator until ganache is firm, about 1 hour. Cut into 16 pieces. Serve.

Calories 390; **fat calories** 170; **total fat** 19g; **sat fat** 8g; **cholesterol** 45mg; **sodium** 170mg **total carbohydrates** 53g; **fiber** 3g; **sugars** 38g; **protein** 5g; **vitamin A IUs** 6%; **vitamin C** 0%; **calcium** 4%; **iron** 8%

CHIPOTLE-CHOCOLATE CAKE WITH VANILLA BUTTERCREAM 🌶🌶

Surprise and delight your guests with this decadent cake.

PREP TIME: **1 HR. 15 MIN**. / TOTAL TIME: **3 HR. 30 MIN.** / SERVES: **12 (1 SLICE)**

Cake

- 2 cups all-purpose flour
- ¾ cup cocoa powder
- 1 teaspoon baking powder
- ⅛ teaspoon salt
- 1 dried chipotle chile pepper, stem and seeds removed, finely ground
- 2 cups granulated sugar
- 12 tablespoons unsalted butter, softened (¾ cup)
- 2 teaspoons pure vanilla extract
- 3 large eggs, room temperature
- 1½ cups whole milk
- 3 ounces dark chocolate, grated (about 1¼ cups)

Buttercream

- 16 tablespoons unsalted butter, softened (1 cup)
- 6 cups powdered sugar, sifted
- ½ cup whole milk
- 2 tablespoons orange zest
- 1 teaspoon pure vanilla extract

1. To make cake, preheat oven to 350°F. Lightly grease 2 (9-inch) round cake pans with butter. Sift flour into a large bowl; sift in cocoa powder and baking powder. Stir in salt and chile.

2. In a bowl, combine granulated sugar, butter, and vanilla; using an electric mixer, mix on medium-low speed until light and fluffy. With mixer on, add eggs, one at a time, mixing well between each. Alternately add flour mixture and milk to butter mixture, starting and ending with flour mixture, mixing on low after each addition, until just combined. Mix in dark chocolate on low speed.

3. Pour batter evenly into prepared pans. Bake at 350°F until a toothpick inserted in center comes out clean, about 40 to 45 minutes. Cool in pans on wire rack 10 minutes. Remove from pans; cool completely on wire rack.

4. To make buttercream, mix butter on medium-low speed until light and fluffy. Mix in powdered sugar, milk, zest, and vanilla on low speed. Frost cake with buttercream. Cut into 12 slices. Serve.

Calories 770; **fat calories** 290; **total fat** 32g; **sat fat** 20g; **cholesterol** 120mg; **sodium** 105mg; **total carbohydrates** 118g; **fiber** 3g; **sugars** 96g; **protein** 6g; **vitamin A IUs** 25%; **vitamin C** 2%; **calcium** 6%; **iron** 15%

CHILE-CHOCOLATE MOLE TRUFFLES 🔥

Ancho

DRIED

Chipotle

DRIED

These truffles are an exotic, subtly spicy, decadent treat.

PREP TIME: **20 MIN.** / TOTAL TIME: **4 HR. 20 MIN.** / SERVES: **36 (1 TRUFFLE)**

10 ounces semi-sweet chocolate chips
1 tablespoon white sesame seeds, toasted
2 tablespoons seedless raisins, minced
5 ounces heavy whipping cream
¼ ounce (about a 1 x 2–inch piece) dried ancho chile pepper
½ teaspoon ground dried chipotle chile pepper
½ teaspoon ground cinnamon
¼ teaspoon fresh lime zest
1 cup walnuts, toasted and finely crushed

1. In a metal bowl, combine chocolate chips, sesame seeds, and raisins. In a small saucepan, heat cream over medium heat; stir in ancho chile, chipotle chile powder, cinnamon, and zest. Bring just to a simmer; immediately remove from heat. Remove and discard ancho; pour cream mixture over chocolate chip mixture, stirring constantly until chocolate is melted and mixture is completely blended. Let cool to room temperature; cover and refrigerate until firm, about 1 to 2 hours.
2. Line a baking sheet with parchment paper. On a plate, spread walnuts in an even layer. Using a ½-teaspoon measuring spoon, scoop out cooled chocolate mixture, form into a 1-inch ball, roll in crushed walnuts, and place on prepared baking sheet. Repeat with remaining chocolate mixture to form 36 truffles. Cover and refrigerate for at least 2 hours, or up to 5 days. Serve.

Calories 80; **fat calories** 50; **total fat** 6g; **sat fat** 2.5g; **cholesterol** 5mg; **sodium** 0mg; **total carbohydrates** 7g; **fiber** 1g; **sugars** 5g; **protein** 1g; **vitamin A IUs** 2%; **vitamin C** 0%; **calcium** 0%; **iron** 2%

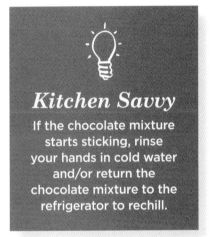

Kitchen Savvy

If the chocolate mixture starts sticking, rinse your hands in cold water and/or return the chocolate mixture to the refrigerator to rechill.

APPLE-CINNAMON-CHILE CRUMB CAKE 》

Guajillo

DRIED

Guajillo chile pepper spices up this traditional fall favorite.

PREP TIME: **1 HOUR** / TOTAL TIME: **2 HR. 35 MIN.** / SERVES: **14 (1 PIECE)**

Apple Topping
- 2 tablespoons unsalted butter
- ½ cup dark rum
- 2 pounds Granny Smith apples, peeled, cored, and sliced
- ⅓ cup granulated sugar
- 2 dried guajillo chile peppers, halved lengthwise, stems and seeds removed

Crumb Topping
- ¾ cup all-purpose flour
- ¼ cup granulated sugar
- ¼ cup packed brown sugar
- 4 tablespoons unsalted butter, melted
- 1 teaspoon ground cinnamon
- ½ teaspoon five-spice powder
- ⅛ teaspoon salt
- 2 dried guajillo chile peppers, stems and seeds removed, ground (about 2 tablespoons)

Cake
- 1½ pounds Granny Smith apples, peeled, cored, and finely diced
- 1 cup plus 2 teaspoons all-purpose flour, divided
- ½ teaspoon baking soda
- ½ teaspoon baking powder
- ½ teaspoon ground cinnamon
- ⅛ teaspoon salt
- ½ cup granulated sugar
- 6 tablespoons unsalted butter, softened
- ⅓ cup plain Greek yogurt
- 1½ tablespoons dark rum
- 1 teaspoon pure vanilla extract
- 1 large whole egg plus 1 large egg yolk
- 2 dried guajillo chile peppers, stems and seeds removed, ground (about 2 tablespoons)

1. To make apple topping, melt butter in a large straight-sided sauté pan over low heat. Add rum and remaining apple topping ingredients; stir until sugar is dissolved. Cook until apple is slightly softened, about 5 minutes. Cool. Remove chile peppers.

2. To make crumb topping, in a bowl, stir together all crumb topping ingredients.

3. To make cake, preheat oven to 350°F. Spray a 9 x 13–inch cake pan with cooking spray. Line pan with parchment paper; spray with cooking spray. In a large bowl, combine finely diced apple and 2 teaspoons flour; toss to coat. In a bowl, sift together remaining 1 cup flour, baking soda, and next 3 ingredients (through salt).

4. In a mixer fitted with a paddle attachment, combine granulated sugar and butter; mix on medium-low speed until light and fluffy, about 3 to 5 minutes. Add yogurt, rum, vanilla, egg, and egg yolk; mix on low speed until thoroughly combined. With mixer on low, gradually add flour mixture and chile to bowl, mixing until just combined. Remove bowl from mixer; fold in diced apple-flour mixture.

5. Pour batter into prepared pan. Top with apple topping; top with crumb topping. Bake at 350°F until a toothpick inserted in center comes out clean, about 50 to 60 minutes. Cool completely. Cut into 14 pieces. Serve.

Calories 310; **fat calories** 80; **total fat** 9g; **sat fat** 5g; **cholesterol** 50mg; **sodium** 75mg; **total carbohydrates** 49g; **fiber** 2g; **sugars** 26g; **protein** 3g; **vitamin A IUs** 25%; **vitamin C** 6%; **calcium** 2%; **iron** 4%

SPICED CHOCOLATE BANANA CREAM PIE 🌶🌶

Hatch

DRIED

Look for refrigerated piecrust shells in the freezer section of your local supermarket.

PREP TIME: **30 MIN.** / TOTAL TIME: **4 HR. 52 MIN.** / SERVES: **10 (1 SLICE)**

- ¾ cup semi-sweet chocolate, chopped (about 4 ounces)
- ¼ cup heavy cream
- 3 tablespoons unsalted butter, divided
- 4 dried Hatch chile peppers, stems and seeds removed, ground (about ¼ cup)
- Purchased piecrust shell
- 3 tablespoons cornstarch
- 1⅓ cups cold water
- 1 14-ounce can sweetened condensed milk
- 3 large egg yolks, beaten
- 2 teaspoons pure vanilla extract
- 2 bananas, cut into ¼-inch-thick slices
- Whipped cream (optional)
- Shaved chocolate (optional)

1. In a large saucepan, combine chocolate, cream, 1 tablespoon butter, and chile; cook over medium heat until melted and smooth, stirring constantly, about 5 minutes. Prepare pie shell according to package directions. Pour chocolate mixture into prepared shell and brush up the sides. Cool until set.

2. In a large saucepan, stir together cornstarch and 1⅓ cups water until cornstarch is dissolved. Stir in condensed milk; add egg yolks. Cook over medium heat until thickened, gently whisking constantly, about 2 to 3 minutes; immediately remove from heat (caution: mixture will thicken rapidly). Strain into a bowl; stir in remaining 2 tablespoons butter and vanilla.

3. Top chocolate mixture in pie shell evenly with half of bananas; top evenly with half of egg mixture. Top evenly with remaining half of bananas; top evenly with remaining half of egg mixture. Refrigerate until set, about 4 hours. Top evenly with whipped cream and chocolate shavings, if desired. Cut into 10 slices. Serve.

Calories 552; **fat calories** 264; **total fat** 29g; **sat fat** 12g; **cholesterol** 84mg; **sodium** 136mg; **total carbohydrates** 64g; **fiber** 2g; **sugars** 37g; **protein** 6g; **vitamin A IUs** 8%; **vitamin C** 3%; **calcium** 12%; **iron** 12%

Simple Swap

Try making this luscious layered pie with a pre-made graham cracker crust or chocolate cookie crust instead of a regular piecrust.

FRESH FRUIT CRUNCH 🌶

Chile peppers in a fruit dessert? It makes sense since, botanically, chiles are berries. Top each serving wtih a scoop of vanilla ice cream.

FRESH

PREP TIME: **25 MIN.** / TOTAL TIME: **55 MIN.** / SERVES: **6 (1 DISH)**

½ cup pomegranate arils
1 tablespoon pure vanilla extract
6 fresh shishito chile peppers, stems and seeds removed, chopped
2 mangos, pitted, peeled, and cubed
2 apples, peeled, cored, and cubed
2 pears, peeled, pitted, and cubed
½ cup old-fashioned oats
½ cup pecan pieces
⅓ cup packed brown sugar
2 tablespoons unsalted butter, melted
½ teaspoon cinnamon

1. Preheat oven to 400°F. In a bowl, combine pomegranate arils and next 5 ingredients (through pears). Spoon fruit mixture evenly into 6 small baking dishes or ramekins.

2. In a bowl, combine oats and remaining ingredients. Top fruit-filled dishes evenly with oat mixture. Arrange dishes on a baking sheet; bake at 400°F until oat mixture is browned and fruit mixture is heated through, about 20 minutes. Let stand 10 minutes. Serve.

Calories 300; **fat calories** 110; **total fat** 12g; **sat fat** 1g; **cholesterol** 0mg; **sodium** 0mg; **total carbohydrates** 48g; **fiber** 6g; **sugars** 36g; **protein** 4g; **vitamin A IUs** 25%; **vitamin C** 100%; **calcium** 4%; **iron** 6%

Simple Swap

This recipe works very well with quince, too: peel, chop, then cook over medium heat until slightly softened before combining with the other fruits.

Thai

FRESH

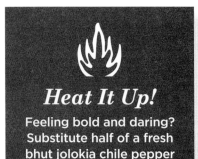

Heat It Up!

Feeling bold and daring? Substitute half of a fresh bhut jolokia chile pepper for the Thai chile peppers.

BAKED STUFFED APPLES 〃

Old-fashioned baked stuffed apples get a sizzling update with dried fruits and fiery Thai chile peppers.

PREP TIME: **30 MIN.** / TOTAL TIME: **1 HR. 25 MIN.** / SERVES: **6 (1 APPLE)**

6 Granny Smith apples
½ cup packed brown sugar
1 teaspoon ground cinnamon
¼ teaspoon ground nutmeg
3 fresh Thai chile peppers, stems and seeds removed, finely chopped
1 3-ounce package dried Bing cherries, chopped
1 3-ounce package dried pineapple chunks
1 3-ounce package dried strawberries, chopped
2 tablespoons unsalted butter
1 cup fresh orange juice

1. Preheat oven to 325°F. Core apples. Using a knife, cut a wide opening, reserving apple pieces. In a bowl, combine brown sugar and next 6 ingredients (through strawberries). Finally chop reserved apple pieces; stir into dried fruit mixture.
2. Fill each apple cavity evenly with fruit mixture and top each with 1 teaspoon butter. Arrange, upright, in a casserole dish.
3. Pour juice around apples; cover with foil. Bake at 325°F until apples are softened, about 45 minutes to 1 hour. Serve.

Calories 350; **fat calories** 35; **total fat** 4g; **sat fat** 2.5g; **cholesterol** 10mg; **sodium** 15mg; **total carbohydrates** 78g; **fiber** 8g; **sugars** 65g; **protein** 1g; **vitamin A IUs** 8%; **vitamin C** 40%; **calcium** 4%; **iron** 4%

GINGER SPICE COOKIES 🌶🌶

The peppery sweet heat of ginger goes beautifully with the smoky velvet heat of chipotle in these quick, easy, egg-free cookies.

PREP TIME: **20 MIN.** / TOTAL TIME: **40 MIN.** / SERVES: **36 (1 COOKIE)**

1½ cups all-purpose flour
1 tablespoon cocoa powder
1 tablespoon baking soda
¼ teaspoon ground nutmeg
8 tablespoons unsalted butter, room temperature (½ cup)
½ cup packed brown sugar
2 dried chipotle chile peppers, stems and seeds removed, finely ground
1 tablespoon water
2 6-ounce packages crystalized ginger (about 1 cup)
2 6-ounce packages dried tart cherries (about 1 cup)
1 1-inch piece fresh ginger, peeled and minced (about 1 tablespoon)
¼ cup granulated sugar

1. Preheat oven to 350°F. Sift together flour, cocoa powder, baking soda, and nutmeg.
2. In a mixer fitted with a paddle attachment, combine butter, brown sugar, and chipotle chile; mix on medium-low speed until light and fluffy. Mix in 1 tablespoon water, crystallized ginger, cherries, and fresh ginger on low speed until combined. With mixer on low, slowly add flour mixture, mixing until combined.
3. Shape dough into 36 (1-inch) balls; roll in granulated sugar. Arrange 2 inches apart on a baking sheet. Bake at 350°F until golden brown, about 10 to 12 minutes. Cool on wire racks. Serve.

Calories 130; **fat calories** 20; **total fat** 2.5g; **sat fat** 1.5g; **cholesterol** 5mg; **sodium** 40mg; **total carbohydrates** 28g; **fiber** 0g; **sugars** 17g; **protein** 1g; **vitamin A IUs** 10%; **vitamin C** 0%; **calcium** 2%; **iron** 2%

MARGARITA CHILE-CHEESECAKE BARS 🌶

For a fun finish, garnish these yummy bars with whipped cream, lime zest curls, and extra ground chile pepper.

PREP TIME: **18 MIN.** / TOTAL TIME: **1 HR.** / SERVES: **16 (1 BAR)**

2 cups graham cracker crumbs
4 tablespoons salted butter, chopped (¼ cup)
6 dried Cascabel chile peppers, stems and seeds removed, ground (about ⅓ cup)
¾ cup non-alcoholic margarita cocktail mix
½ cup plus 1 tablespoon granulated sugar
2½ tablespoons cornstarch
3 tablespoons lime zest
2 8-ounce packages cream cheese, softened
2 large eggs

1. Preheat oven to 350°F. Place graham cracker crumbs, butter, and chile in a food processor; pulse until coarse and crumbly, about 2 minutes. Transfer graham-cracker mixture to a 13 x 9 x 2–inch baking dish; press to evenly cover bottom of dish. Bake at 350°F until golden, about 12 to 15 minutes. Cool.
2. In a bowl, combine margarita mix and next 4 ingredients (through cream cheese). Whisk in eggs until completely incorporated. Pour over crust; bake until top browns slightly, about 30 minutes. Cool completely in pan. Cut into 16 bars. Serve.

Calories 270; **fat calories** 150; **total fat** 17g; **sat fat** 9g; **cholesterol** 0mg; **sodium** 210mg; **total carbohydrates** 28g; **fiber** 0g; **sugars** 17g; **protein** 3g; **vitamin A IUs** 20%; **vitamin C** 2%; **calcium** 4%; **iron** 4%

thank you!

First, to the creative Melissa's chef team led by Executive Chef **Ida Rodriguez** and Test Kitchen director **Chef Tom Fraker,** along with **Raquel Perez** and **Nancy Eisman:** We thank you for embracing the wonderful flavors of every pepper and creating recipes that reflect their flair. To produce guru **Robert Schueller:** Thank you for all your input and unending knowledge about peppers. A special thanks goes to **Debra Cohen,** along with well-known nutritionist **Cheryl Forberg, R.D.,** and **David Feder, R.D.N.,** for their help in reviewing every recipe detail. Finally, thank you to the brilliant team at **Oxmoor House,** including editor **Meredith Butcher** as well as **Becky Luigart-Stayner, Ana Price Kelly, Mary Clayton Carl, J. Shay McNamee, Lacie Pinyan,** and brand manager **Vanessa Tiongson.**

Sharon and Joe Hernandez,
Owners & Visionaries of Melissa's Produce

about Melissa's

Melissa's / World Variety Produce, Inc. is currently the largest distributor of specialty produce in the United States. Produce pioneers and company founders Sharon and Joe Hernandez named the company after their daughter, and over the past few decades have introduced exotic, conventional, and organic produce items from around the globe.

Melissa's has long been recognized as the extraordinary supplier for the freshest fruits and vegetables, and the company prides themselves on providing quality products with exceptional value and first-class service.

Melissa's consistently shares what's in season with you, to bring the flavors of the world to your kitchen. Please visit us at **www.melissas.com** and be sure to look and ask for Melissa's brand in your local produce department.

Nutritional Information

Daily Nutrition Guide

	Women ages 25 to 50	Women over 50	Men ages 24 to 50	Men over 50
Calories	2,000	2,000 or less	2,700	2,500
Protein	50g	50g or less	63g	60g
Fat	65g or less	65g or less	88g or less	83g or less
Saturated Fat	20g or less	20g or less	27g or less	25g or less
Carbohydrates	304g	304g	410g	375g
Fiber	25g to 35g	25g to 35g	25g to 35g	25g to 35g
Cholesterol	300mg or less	300mg or less	300mg or less	300mg or less
Iron	18mg	8mg	8mg	8mg
Sodium	2,300mg or less	1,500mg or less	2,300mg or less	1,500mg or less
Calcium	1,000mg	1,200mg	1,000mg	1,000mg

Metric Equivalents

The information in the following charts is provided to help cooks outside the United States successfully use the recipes in this book. All equivalents are approximate.

Cooking/Oven Temperatures

	Fahrenheit	Celsius	Gas Mark
Freeze Water	32° F	0° C	
Room Temp.	68° F	20° C	
Boil Water	212° F	100° C	
Bake	325° F	160° C	3
	350° F	180° C	4
	375° F	190° C	5
	400° F	200° C	6
	425° F	220° C	7
	450° F	230° C	8
Broil			Grill

Liquid Ingredients by Volume

¼ tsp	=				1 ml
½ tsp	=				2 ml
1 tsp	=				5 ml
3 tsp	=	1 Tbsp =	½ fl oz =		15 ml
2 Tbsp =		⅛ cup =	1 fl oz =		30 ml
4 Tbsp =		¼ cup =	2 fl oz =		60 ml
5⅓ Tbsp =		⅓ cup =	3 fl oz =		80 ml
8 Tbsp =		½ cup =	4 fl oz =		120 ml
10⅔ Tbsp =		⅔ cup =	5 fl oz =		160 ml
12 Tbsp =		¾ cup =	6 fl oz =		180 ml
16 Tbsp =		1 cup =	8 fl oz =		240 ml
1 pt	=	2 cups =	16 fl oz =		480 ml
1 qt	=	4 cups =	32 fl oz =		960 ml
			33 fl oz =	1000 ml	= 1 l

Equivalents for Different Types of Ingredients

Standard Cup	Fine Powder (ex. flour)	Grain (ex. rice)	Granular (ex. sugar)	Liquid Solids (ex. butter)	Liquid (ex. milk)
1	140 g	150 g	190 g	200 g	240 ml
¾	105 g	113 g	143 g	150 g	180 ml
⅔	93 g	100 g	125 g	133 g	160 ml
½	70 g	75 g	95 g	100 g	120 ml
⅓	47 g	50 g	63 g	67 g	80 ml
¼	35 g	38 g	48 g	50 g	60 ml
⅛	18 g	19 g	24 g	25 g	30 ml

Dry Ingredients by Weight

(To convert ounces to grams, multiply the number of ounces by 30.)

1 oz	=	¹⁄₁₆ lb	=	30 g
4 oz	=	¼ lb	=	120 g
8 oz	=	½ lb	=	240 g
12 oz	=	¾ lb	=	360 g
16 oz	=	1 lb	=	480 g

Length

(To convert inches to centimeters, multiply the number of inches by 2.5.)

1 in	=					2.5 cm
6 in	=	½ ft		=		15 cm
12 in	=	1 ft		=		30 cm
36 in	=	3 ft	= 1 yd	=		90 cm
40 in	=					100 cm = 1 m

index

a

b

c

Hardcover
ISBN-13: 978-0-8487-0446-9
ISBN-10: 0-8487-0446-0
Softcover
ISBN-13: 978-0-8487-0431-5
ISBN-10: 0-8487-0431-2
Custom Melissa's edition
ISBN-13: 978-0-8487-4426-7
ISBN-10: 0-8487-4426-8

Library of Congress Control Number: 2014930618

Printed in the United States of America
First Printing 2014

Melissa's Team

Owners: Sharon and Joe Hernandez
Executive Chef: Ida Rodriguez
Test Kitchen Director: Tom Fraker
Test Kitchen Chef: Raquel Perez
Director of Public Relations: Robert Schueller
Recipe Liaison, Special Projects: Nancy Eisman
Organizational Liaison, Special Projects:
    Debra Cohen
Editorial Consultant: David P.B. Feder, R.D.N.
Nutrition Editor: Cheryl Forberg, R.D.

Oxmoor House

Vice President, Brand Publishing: Laura Sappington
Editorial Director: Leah McLaughlin
Creative Director: Felicity Keane
Brand Manager: Vanessa Tiongson
Senior Editor: Andrea C. Kirkland, M.S., R.D.
Managing Editor: Elizabeth Tyler Austin
Assistant Managing Editor: Jeanne de Lathouder

Melissa's The Great Pepper Cookbook

Editor: Meredith L. Butcher
Art Director: Christopher Rhoads
Project Editor: Lacie Pinyan
Senior Designer: J. Shay McNamee
Executive Food Director: Grace Parisi
Assistant Test Kitchen Manager:
    Alyson Moreland Haynes
Recipe Developers and Testers: Wendy Ball, R.D.;
    Tamara Goldis, R.D.; Stefanie Maloney;
    Callie Nash; Karen Rankin; Leah Van Deren
Food Stylists: Victoria E. Cox, Margaret Monroe Dickey,
    Catherine Crowell Steele
Photography Director: Jim Bathie
Senior Photographer: Hélène Dujardin
Senior Photo Stylist: Kay E. Clarke
Photo Stylist: Mindi Shapiro Levine
Assistant Photo Stylist: Mary Louise Menendez
Production Manager: Theresa Beste-Farley
Associate Production Manager: Kimberly Marshall

Contributors

Compositor: Carol Damsky
Copy Editors: Erica Midkiff, Deri Reed
Indexer: Mary Ann Laurens
Fellows: Ali Carruba, Frances Higginbotham,
    Elizabeth Laseter, Amy Pinney, Madison Taylor
    Pozzo, Deanna Sakal, April Smitherman,
    Megan Thompson, Tonya West
Food Stylist: Ana Price Kelly
Photographer: Becky Luigart-Stayner
Photo Stylist: Mary Clayton Carl

Time Home Entertainment Inc.

Publisher: Jim Childs
Vice President, Brand & Digital Strategy:
    Steven Sandonato
Executive Director, Marketing Services:
    Carol Pittard
Executive Director, Retail & Special Sales:
    Tom Mifsud
Director, Bookazine Development & Marketing:
    Laura Adam
Executive Publishing Director: Joy Butts
Publishing Director: Megan Pearlman
Finance Director: Glenn Buonocore
Associate General Counsel: Helen Wan